WISDOM KEYS MI... ...CK ©

WISDOM KEY#	WISDOM KEY	...SCRIPTURES ON THE WORD OF GOD
1	**Every Problem Is Always A Wisdom Problem.**	**JANUARY 1 /** *Genesis 1-3* Sojourn in this land, and I will be with thee, and will bless thee; for unto thee, and unto thy seed, I will give all these countries, and I will perform the oath which I sware unto Abraham thy father; Because that Abraham obeyed My voice, and kept My charge, My commandments, My statutes, and My laws. (Genesis 26:3,5)
2	**When Your Heart Decides The Destination, Your Mind Will Design The Map To Reach It.**	**JANUARY 2 /** *Genesis 4-6* And said, If thou wilt diligently hearken to the voice of the Lord thy God, and wilt do that which is right in His sight, and wilt give ear to His commandments, and keep all His statutes, I will put none of these diseases upon thee, which I have brought upon the Egyptians: for I am the Lord that healeth thee. (Exodus 15:26)
3	**Whatever You Respect, You Will Attract.**	**JANUARY 3 /** *Genesis 7-9* Now therefore, if ye will obey My voice indeed, and keep My covenant, then ye shall be a peculiar treasure unto Me above all people: for all the earth is Mine: (Exodus 19:5)
4	**The Secret Of Your Future Is Hidden In Your Daily Routine.**	**JANUARY 4 /** *Genesis 10-14* And the Lord said unto Moses, Come up to Me into the mount, and be there: and I will give thee tables of stone, and a law, and commandments which I have written; that thou mayest teach them. (Exodus 24:12)
5	**Your Rewards In Life Are Determined By The Kinds Of Problems You Are Willing To Solve For Others.**	**JANUARY 5 /** *Genesis 15-17* Ye shall therefore keep My statutes, and My judgments: which if a man do, he shall live in them: I am the Lord. (Leviticus 18:5)
6	**What You Make Happen For Others, God Will Make Happen For You.**	**JANUARY 6 /** *Genesis 18-20* Ye shall therefore keep all My statutes, and all My judgments, and do them: that the land, whither I bring you to dwell therein, spue you not out. (Leviticus 20:22)
7	**An Uncommon Seed Always Creates An Uncommon Harvest.**	**JANUARY 7 /** *Genesis 21-23* Wherefore ye shall do My statutes, and keep My judgments, and do them; and ye shall dwell in the land in safety. And the land shall yield her fruit, and ye shall eat your fill, and dwell therein in safety. (Leviticus 25:18,19)

WISDOM KEYS OF
MIKE MURDOCK ©

WISDOM KEY#	WISDOM KEY	MEMORY SCRIPTURES ON THE WORD OF GOD
8	**The Word Of God Is The Wisdom Of God.**	***JANUARY 8** / Genesis 24-26* If ye walk in My statutes, and keep My commandments, and do them; Then I will give you rain in due season, and the land shall yield her increase, and the trees of the field shall yield their fruit. (Leviticus 26:3,4)
9	**The Clearer Your Goals, The Greater Your Faith.**	***JANUARY 9** / Genesis 27-29* If ye walk in My statutes, and keep My commandments, and do them; And your threshing shall reach unto the vintage, and the vintage shall reach unto the sowing time: and ye shall eat your bread to the full, and dwell in your land safely. (Leviticus 26:3,5)
10	**Your Focus Decides Your Feelings.**	***JANUARY 10** / Genesis 30-32* If ye walk in My statutes, and keep My commandments, and do them; And ye shall chase your enemies, and they shall fall before you by the sword. (Leviticus 26:3,7)
11	**Your Self-Portrait Determines Your Self-Conduct.**	***JANUARY 11** / Genesis 33-37* If ye walk in My statutes, and keep My commandments, and do them; For I will have respect unto you, and make you fruitful, and multiply you, and establish My covenant with you. (Leviticus 26:3,9)
12	**Your Respect For Time Is A Prediction Of Your Financial Future.**	***JANUARY 12** / Genesis 38-40* If ye walk in My statutes, and keep My commandments, and do them; And I will walk among you, and will be your God, and ye shall be My people. (Leviticus 26:3,12)
13	**Your Decisions Decide Your Wealth.**	***JANUARY 13** / Genesis 41-43* But if ye will not hearken unto Me, and will not do all these commandments; I also will do this unto you; I will even appoint over you terror, consumption, and the burning ague, that shall consume the eyes, and cause sorrow of heart: and ye shall sow your seed in vain, for your enemies shall eat it. (Leviticus 26:14,16)
14	**The Instruction You Follow Determines The Future You Create.**	***JANUARY 14** / Genesis 44-46* But if ye will not hearken unto Me, and will not do all these commandments; Then will I also walk contrary unto you, and will punish you yet seven times for your sins. (Leviticus 26:14,24)

WISDOM KEYS OF
MIKE MURDOCK ©

WISDOM KEY#	WISDOM KEY	MEMORY SCRIPTURES ON THE WORD OF GOD
15	God's Only Pain Is To Be Doubted; God's Only Pleasure Is To Be Believed.	**JANUARY 15** / *Genesis 47-49* Because he hath despised the word of the Lord, and hath broken His commandment, that soul shall utterly be cut off; His iniquity shall be upon him. (Numbers 15:31)
16	Your Goals Choose Your Mentors.	**JANUARY 16** / *Genesis 50 - Exodus 2* God is not a man, that He should lie; neither the son of man, that He should repent: hath He said, and shall He not do it? or hath He spoken, and shall He not make it good? (Numbers 23:19)
17	Your Success Is Decided By What You Are Willing To Ignore.	**JANUARY 17** / *Exodus 3-5* Ye shall not add unto the word which I command you, neither shall ye diminish ought from it, that ye may keep the commandments of the Lord your God which I command you. (Deuteronomy 4:2)
18	The Atmosphere You Create Determines The Product You Produce.	**JANUARY 18** / *Exodus 6-10* Keep therefore and do them; for this is your wisdom and your understanding in the sight of the nations, which shall hear all these statutes, and say, Surely this great nation is a wise and understanding people. (Deuteronomy 4:6)
19	The Size Of Your Enemy Determines The Size Of Your Rewards.	**JANUARY 19** / *Exodus 11-13* Only take heed to thyself, and keep thy soul diligently, lest thou forget the things which thine eyes have seen, and lest they depart from thy heart all the days of thy life: but teach them thy sons, and thy sons` sons; (Deuteronomy 4:9)
20	Your Assignment Is Always The Problem God Has Designed You To Solve For Others.	**JANUARY 20** / *Exodus 14-16* Specially the day that thou stoodest before the Lord thy God in Horeb, when the Lord said unto me, Gather Me the people together, and I will make them hear My words, that they may learn to fear Me all the days that they shall live upon the earth, and that they may teach their children. (Deuteronomy 4:10)
21	What You Are Willing To Walk Away From Determines What God Will Bring To You.	**JANUARY 21** / *Exodus 17-19* And He declared unto you His covenant, which He commanded you to perform, even ten commandments; and He wrote them upon two tables of stone. (Deuteronomy 4:13)

WISDOM KEYS OF
MIKE MURDOCK ©

WISDOM KEY#	WISDOM KEY	MEMORY SCRIPTURES ON THE WORD OF GOD
22	Your Future Is Decided By Who You Choose To Believe.	**JANUARY 22** / *Exodus 20-22* And the Lord commanded me at that time to teach you statutes and judgments, that ye might do them in the land whither ye go over to possess it. (Deuteronomy 4:14)
23	Changes In Your Life Will Always Be Proportionate To Your Knowledge.	**JANUARY 23** / *Exodus 23-25* Take heed unto yourselves, lest ye forget the covenant of the Lord your God, which He made with you, (Deuteronomy 4:23a)
24	The Reward Of Pain Is The Willingness To Change.	**JANUARY 24** / *Exodus 26-28* When thou art in tribulation, and all these things are come upon thee, even in the latter days, if thou turn to the Lord thy God, and shalt be obedient unto His voice; (For the Lord thy God is a merciful God;) He will not forsake thee, neither destroy thee, nor forget the covenant of thy fathers which He sware unto them. (Deut. 4:30,31)
25	Anything Permitted Increases.	**JANUARY 25** / *Exodus 29-33* Out of heaven He made thee to hear His voice, that He might instruct thee: and upon earth He shewed thee his great fire; and thou heardest His words out of the midst of the fire. (Deuteronomy 4:36)
26	Anything That Keeps Your Attention Has Become Your Master.	**JANUARY 26** / *Exodus 34-36* Thou shalt keep therefore His statutes, and His commandments, which I command thee this day, that it may go well with thee, and with thy children after thee, and that thou mayest prolong thy days upon the earth, which the Lord thy God giveth thee, for ever. (Deuteronomy 4:40)
27	Your Life Is Whatever You Choose To Remember.	**JANUARY 27** / *Exodus 37-39* And Moses called all Israel, and said unto them, Hear, O Israel, the statutes and judgments which I speak in your ears this day, that ye may learn them, and keep, and do them. (Deuteronomy 5:1)
28	When You Want Something You Have Never Had, You Must Do Something You Have Never Done.	**JANUARY 28** / *Exodus 40 - Leviticus 2* O that there were such an heart in them, that they would fear Me, and keep all My commandments always, that it might be well with them, and with their children for ever! (Deuteronomy 5:29)

WISDOM KEYS OF
MIKE MURDOCK©

WISDOM KEY#	WISDOM KEY	MEMORY SCRIPTURES ON THE WORD OF GOD
29	**What You Repeatedly Hear, You Eventually Believe.**	**JANUARY 29 /** *Leviticus 3-5* Ye shall observe to do therefore as the Lord your God hath commanded you: ye shall not turn aside to the right hand or to the left. (Deuteronomy 5:32)
30	**All Men Fall; The Great Ones Get Back Up.**	**JANUARY 30 /** *Leviticus 6-8* Ye shall walk in all the ways which the Lord your God hath commanded you, that ye may live, and that it may be well with you, and that ye may prolong your days in the land which ye shall possess. (Deuteronomy 5:33)
31	**You Cannot Correct What You Are Unwilling To Confront.**	**JANUARY 31 /** *Leviticus 9-11* That thou mightest fear the Lord thy God, to keep all His statutes and His commandments, which I command thee, thou, and thy son, and thy son`s son, all the days of thy life; and that thy days may be prolonged. (Deuteronomy 6:2)
32	**You Will Only Be Remembered In Life For Two Things: The Problems You Solve Or The Ones You Create.**	**FEBRUARY 1 /** *Leviticus 12-16* And these words, which I command thee this day, shall be in thine heart: And thou shalt teach them diligently unto thy children, and shalt talk of them when thou sittest in thine house, and when thou walkest by the way, and when thou liest down, and when thou risest up. (Deuteronomy 6:6,7)
33	**God Never Consults Your Past To Decide Your Future.**	**FEBRUARY 2 /** *Leviticus 17-19* And these words, which I command thee this day, shall be in thine heart: And thou shalt bind them for a sign upon thine hand, and they shall be as frontlets between thine eyes. (Deuteronomy 6:6,8)
34	**Any Movement Towards Order Creates Pleasure.**	**FEBRUARY 3 /** *Leviticus 20-22* And these words, which I command thee this day, shall be in thine heart: And thou shalt write them upon the posts of thy house, and on thy gates. (Deuteronomy 6:6,9)
35	**If You Insist On Taking Something God Did Not Give You, He Will Take Back Something He Gave You.**	**FEBRUARY 4 /** *Leviticus 23-25* And the Lord commanded us to do all these statutes, to fear the Lord our God, for our good always, that He might preserve us alive, as it is at this day. (Deuteronomy 6:24)

WISDOM KEYS OF MIKE MURDOCK ©

WISDOM KEY#	WISDOM KEY	MEMORY SCRIPTURES ON THE WORD OF GOD
36	The Evidence Of God's Presence Far Outweighs The Proof Of His Absence.	**FEBRUARY 5** / *Leviticus 26 - Numbers 1* Know therefore that the Lord thy God, He is God, the faithful God, which keepeth covenant and mercy with them that love Him and keep His commandments to a thousand generations; (Deuteronomy 7:9)
37	Never Complain About What You Permit.	**FEBRUARY 6** / *Numbers 2-4* Wherefore it shall come to pass, if ye hearken to these judgments, and keep, and do them, that the Lord thy God shall keep unto thee the covenant and the mercy which He sware unto thy fathers: And He will love thee, and bless thee, and multiply thee: He will also bless the fruit of thy womb, and the fruit of thy land, thy corn, and thy wine, and thine oil, the increase of thy kine, and the flocks of thy sheep, in the land which He sware unto thy fathers to give thee. (Deuteronomy 7:12,13)
38	Go Where You Are Celebrated Instead Of Where You Are Tolerated.	**FEBRUARY 7** / *Numbers 5-7* Wherefore it shall come to pass, if ye hearken to these judgments, and keep, and do them,...And the Lord will take away from thee all sickness, and will put none of the evil diseases of Egypt, which thou knowest, upon thee; but will lay them upon all them that hate thee. (Deuteronomy 7:12,a,15)
39	One Day Of Favor Is Worth A Thousand Days Of Labor.	**FEBRUARY 8** / *Numbers 8-12* And He humbled thee, and suffered thee to hunger, and fed thee with manna, which thou knewest not, neither did thy fathers know; that He might make thee know that man doth not live by bread only, but by every word that proceedeth out of the mouth of the Lord doth man live. (Deuteronomy 8:3)
40	Warfare Always Surrounds The Birth Of A Miracle.	**FEBRUARY 9** / *Numbers 13-15* And now, Israel, what doth the Lord thy God require of thee, but to fear the Lord thy God, to walk in all His ways, and to love Him, and to serve the Lord thy God with all thy heart and with all thy soul, To keep the commandments of the Lord, and His statutes, which I command thee this day for thy good? (Deuteronomy 10:12,13)
41	The Broken Become Masters At Mending.	**FEBRUARY 10** / *Numbers 16-18* Therefore thou shalt love the Lord thy God, and keep His charge, and His statutes, and His judgments, and His commandments, alway. (Deuteronomy 11:1)
42	Prosperity Is Simply Having Enough Of God's Provision To Complete His Assignment In Your Life.	**FEBRUARY 11** / *Numbers 19-21* Therefore shall ye keep all the commandments which I command you this day, that ye may be strong, and go in and possess the land, whither ye go to possess it; (Deuteronomy 11:8)

WISDOM KEYS OF
MIKE MURDOCK©

WISDOM KEY#	WISDOM KEY	MEMORY SCRIPTURES ON THE WORD OF GOD
43	**One Hour In The Presence Of God Will Reveal The Flaws Of Your Most Carefully Laid Plans.**	**FEBRUARY 12** / *Numbers 22-24* And it shall come to pass, if ye shall hearken diligently unto My commandments which I command you this day, to love the Lord your God, and to serve Him with all your heart and with all your soul, That I will give you the rain of your land in His due season, the first rain and the latter rain, that thou mayest gather in thy corn, and thy wine, and thine oil. (Deuteronomy 11:13,14)
44	**Anger Is The Birthplace For Solutions.**	**FEBRUARY 13** / *Numbers 25-27* And it shall come to pass, if ye shall hearken diligently unto My commandments which I command you this day,...And I will send grass in thy fields for thy cattle, that thou mayest eat and be full. (Deuteronomy 11:13a,15)
45	**The Willingness To Reach Births The Ability To Change.**	**FEBRUARY 14** / *Numbers 28-30* Therefore shall ye lay up these My words in your heart and in your soul, and bind them for a sign upon your hand, that they may be as frontlets between your eyes. (Deuteronomy 11:18)
46	**Never Give More Time To A Critic Than You Would Give To A Friend.**	**FEBRUARY 15** / *Numbers 31-35* And ye shall teach them your children, speaking of them when thou sittest in thine house, and when thou walkest by the way, when thou liest down, and when thou risest up. (Deuteronomy 11:19)
47	**Access Is First A Gift, Then A Test, Then A Reward.**	**FEBRUARY 16** / *Numbers 36 - Deuteronomy 2* For if ye shall diligently keep all these commandments which I command you, to do them, to love the Lord your God, to walk in all His ways, and to cleave unto Him; Then will the Lord drive out all these nations from before you, and ye shall possess greater nations and mightier than yourselves. (Deuteronomy 11:22,23)
48	**The Magnetism Of Your Kindness Will Outlast The Memory Of Your Genius.**	**FEBRUARY 17** / *Deuteronomy 3-5* For if ye shall diligently keep all these commandments which I command you, to do them, to love the Lord your God, to walk in all His ways, and to cleave unto Him; There shall no man be able to stand before you: for the Lord your God shall lay the fear of you and the dread of you upon all the land that ye shall tread upon, as He hath said unto you. (Deuteronomy 11:22,25)
49	**When You Let Go Of What's In Your Hand, God Will Let Go Of What's In His Hand.**	**FEBRUARY 18** / *Deuteronomy 6-8* Behold, I set before you this day a blessing and a curse; A blessing, if ye obey the commandments of the Lord your God, which I command you this day: (Deuteronomy 11:26,27)

WISDOM KEYS OF
MIKE MURDOCK©

WISDOM KEY#	WISDOM KEY	MEMORY SCRIPTURES ON THE WORD OF GOD
50	Never Rewrite Your Theology To Accommodate A Tragedy.	**FEBRUARY 19 /** *Deuteronomy 9-11* And a curse, if ye will not obey the commandments of the Lord your God, but turn aside out of the way which I command you this day, to go after other gods, which ye have not known. (Deuteronomy 11:28)
51	Crisis Always Occurs At The Curve Of Change.	**FEBRUARY 20 /** *Deuteronomy 12-14* Observe and hear all these words which I command thee, that it may go well with thee, and with thy children after thee for ever, when thou doest that which is good and right in the sight of the Lord thy God. (Deuteronomy 12:28)
52	You Never Outgrow Warfare; You Must Simply Learn To Fight.	**FEBRUARY 21 /** *Deuteronomy 15-17* What thing soever I command you, observe to do it: thou shalt not add thereto, nor diminish from it. (Deuteronomy 12:32)
53	Memory Is More Enslaving Than Any Injustice.	**FEBRUARY 22 /** *Deuteronomy 18-22* Save when there shall be no poor among you; for the Lord shall greatly bless thee in the land which the Lord thy God giveth thee for an inheritance to possess it: Only if thou carefully hearken unto the voice of the Lord thy God, to observe to do all these commandments which I command thee this day. For the Lord thy God blesseth thee, as He promised thee: and thou shalt lend unto many nations, but thou shalt not borrow; and thou shalt reign over many nations, but they shall not reign over thee. (Deuteronomy 15:4-6)
54	Your Significance Is Not In Your Similarity To Another, But In Your Point Of Difference From Another.	**FEBRUARY 23 /** *Deuteronomy 23-25* And it shall be with him, and he shall read therein all the days of his life: that he may learn to fear the Lord his God, to keep all the words of this law and these statutes, to do them: (Deuteronomy 17:19)
55	What You Can Tolerate You Cannot Change.	**FEBRUARY 24 /** *Deuteronomy 26-28* And it shall be with him, and he shall read therein all the days of his life: that he may learn to fear the Lord his God, to keep all the words of this law and these statutes, to do them: That his heart be not lifted up above his brethren, and that he turn not aside from the commandment, to the right hand, or to the left: to the end that he may prolong his days in his kingdom, he, and his children, in the midst of Israel. (Deuteronomy 17:19,20)
56	The Seasons Of Your Life Will Change Every Time You Use Your Faith.	**FEBRUARY 25 /** *Deuteronomy 29-31* This day the Lord thy God hath commanded thee to do these statutes and judgments: thou shalt therefore keep and do them with all thine heart, and with all thy soul. (Deuteronomy 26:16)

WISDOM KEYS OF
MIKE MURDOCK ©

WISDOM KEY#	WISDOM KEY	MEMORY SCRIPTURES ON THE WORD OF GOD
57	When You Ask God For A Miracle, He Will Always Give You An Instruction.	**FEBRUARY 26 /** *Deuteronomy 32-34* And the Lord hath avouched thee this day to be His peculiar people, as He hath promised thee, and that thou shouldest keep all His commandments; And to make thee high above all nations which He hath made, in praise, and in name, and in honour; and that thou mayest be an holy people unto the Lord thy God, as He hath spoken. (Deuteronomy 26:18,19)
58	Whatever Is Missing In Your Life Is Something You Have Not Truly Valued.	**FEBRUARY 27 /** *Joshua 1-3* Cursed be he that confirmeth not all the words of this law to do them. And all the people shall say, Amen. (Deuteronomy 27:26)
59	Your Reaction To Greatness Reveals Your Humility.	**FEBRUARY 28 /** *Joshua 4-6* And it shall come to pass, if thou shalt hearken diligently unto the voice of the Lord thy God, to observe and to do all His commandments which I command thee this day, that the Lord thy God will set thee on high above all nations of the earth: (Deuteronomy 28:1)
60	Honor Is The Seed For Longevity.	**MARCH 1 /** *Joshua 7-11* And all these blessings shall come on thee, and overtake thee, if thou shalt hearken unto the voice of the Lord thy God. (Deuteronomy 28:2)
61	Your Words Are The Seeds For Feelings.	**MARCH 2 /** *Joshua 12-14* And all these blessings shall come on thee, and overtake thee, if thou shalt hearken unto the voice of the Lord thy God. Blessed shalt thou be in the city, and blessed shalt thou be in the field. (Deuteronomy 28:2,3)
62	Friends Create Comfort; Enemies Create Change.	**MARCH 3 /** *Joshua 15-17* And the Lord shall make thee the head, and not the tail; and thou shalt be above only, and thou shalt not be beneath; if that thou hearken unto the commandments of the Lord thy God, which I command thee this day, to observe and to do them: (Deuteronomy 28:13)
63	Something In Your Hand Can Create Anything You Want In Your Future.	**MARCH 4 /** *Joshua 18-20* But it shall come to pass, if thou wilt not hearken unto the voice of the Lord thy God, to observe to do all His commandments and His statutes which I command thee this day; that all these curses shall come upon thee, and overtake thee: (Deuteronomy 28:15)

WISDOM KEYS OF
MIKE MURDOCK©

WISDOM KEY#	WISDOM KEY	MEMORY SCRIPTURES ON THE WORD OF GOD
64	**Your Unwillingness To Trust The Right Person Will Create More Losses Than Your Mistake Of Trusting The Wrong Person.**	**MARCH 5 /** *Joshua 21-23* And shalt return unto the Lord thy God, and shalt obey His voice according to all that I command thee this day, thou and thy children, with all thine heart, and with all thy soul; That then the Lord thy God will turn thy captivity, and have compassion upon thee, and will return and gather thee from all the nations, whither the Lord thy God hath scattered thee. (Deuteronomy 30:2,3)
65	**Anything Good Is Hated By Everything Evil.**	**MARCH 6 /** *Joshua 24 - Judges 2* And thou shalt return and obey the voice of the Lord, and do all His commandments which I command thee this day. And the Lord thy God will make thee plenteous in every work of thine hand, in the fruit of thy body, and in the fruit of thy cattle, and in the fruit of thy land, for good: for the Lord will again rejoice over thee for good, as He rejoiced over thy fathers: (Deuteronomy 30:8,9)
66	**An Uncommon Dream Will Require An Uncommon Mentor.**	**MARCH 7 /** *Judges 3-5* That thou mayest love the Lord thy God, and that thou mayest obey His voice, and that thou mayest cleave unto Him: for He is thy life, and the length of thy days: that thou mayest dwell in the land which the Lord sware unto thy fathers, to Abraham, to Isaac, and to Jacob, to give them. (Deuteronomy 30:20)
67	**What Saddens You Is A Clue To What God Has Assigned You To Heal.**	**MARCH 8 /** *Judges 6-10* Gather the people together, men, and women, and children, and thy stranger that is within thy gates, that they may hear, and that they may learn, and fear the Lord your God, and observe to do all the words of this law: (Deuteronomy 31:12)
68	**Every Environment Requires A Code Of Conduct For Entering Or Remaining In It.**	**MARCH 9 /** *Judges 11-13* And he said unto them, Set your hearts unto all the words which I testify among you this day, which ye shall command your children to observe to do, all the words of this law. For it is not a vain thing for you; because it is your life: and through this thing ye shall prolong your days in the land, whither ye go over Jordan to possess it. (Deuteronomy 32:46,47)
69	**Greatness Is Not The Absence Of A Flaw— But The Willingness To Overcome It.**	**MARCH 10 /** *Judges 14-16* Only be thou strong and very courageous, that thou mayest observe to do according to all the law, which Moses My servant commanded thee: turn not from it to the right hand or to the left, that thou mayest prosper whithersoever thou goest. (Joshua 1:7)
70	**Each Act Of Obedience Shortens The Distance To Any Miracle You Are Pursuing.**	**MARCH 11 /** *Judges 17-19* This book of the law shall not depart out of thy mouth; but thou shalt meditate therein day and night, that thou mayest observe to do according to all that is written therein: for then thou shalt make thy way prosperous, and then thou shalt have good success. (Joshua 1:8)

WISDOM KEYS OF
MIKE MURDOCK©

WISDOM KEY#	WISDOM KEY	MEMORY SCRIPTURES ON THE WORD OF GOD
71	**Your Reaction To The Word Of God Is A Picture Of Your Respect For God.**	**MARCH 12** / *Judges 20 - Ruth 1* There failed not ought of any good thing which the Lord had spoken unto the house of Israel; all came to pass. (Joshua 21:45)
72	**The Problem That Infuriates You The Most Is The Problem God Has Assigned You To Solve.**	**MARCH 13** / *Ruth 2-4* But if ye will not obey the voice of the Lord, but rebel against the commandment of the Lord, then shall the hand of the Lord be against you, as it was against your fathers. (1 Samuel 12:15)
73	**False Accusation Is The Last Season Before Supernatural Promotion.**	**MARCH 14** / *1 Samuel 1-3* And now, O Lord God, Thou art that God, and Thy words be true, and Thou hast promised this goodness unto Thy servant. (2 Samuel 7:28)
74	**Miracles Happen As Quickly As Tragedies.**	**MARCH 15** / *1 Samuel 4-8* And keep the charge of the Lord thy God, to walk in His ways, to keep His statutes, and His commandments, and His judgments, and His testimonies, as it is written in the law of Moses, that thou mayest prosper in all that thou doest, and whithersoever thou turnest thyself: That the Lord may continue His word which He spake concerning me, saying, If thy children take heed to their way, to walk before Me in truth with all their heart and with all their soul, there shall not fail thee (said He) a man on the throne of Israel. (1 Kings 2:3,4)
75	**The Difference Between Significance And Insignificance Is An Adversary.**	**MARCH 16** / *1 Samuel 9-11* Blessed be the Lord, that hath given rest unto His people Israel, according to all that He promised: there hath not failed one word of all His good promise, which He promised by the hand of Moses His servant. (1 Kings 8:56)
76	**When Wrong People Leave Your Life, Wrong Things Stop Happening.**	**MARCH 17** / *1 Samuel 12-14* And he answered, I have not troubled Israel; but thou, and thy father's house, in that ye have forsaken the commandments of the Lord, and thou hast followed Baalim. (1 Kings 18:18)
77	**Seed-Faith Is Sowing Something You Have Been Given For Something Else You Have Been Promised.**	**MARCH 18** / *1 Samuel 15-17* Yet the Lord testified against Israel, and against Judah, by all the prophets, and by all the seers, saying, Turn ye from your evil ways, and keep My commandments and My statutes, according to all the law which I commanded your fathers, and which I sent to you by My servants the prophets. (2 Kings 17:13)

WISDOM KEYS OF
MIKE MURDOCK©

WISDOM KEY#	WISDOM KEY	MEMORY SCRIPTURES ON THE WORD OF GOD
78	**Disobedience Is Always More Costly Than Obedience.**	**MARCH 19** / *1 Samuel 18-20* Moreover I will establish his kingdom for ever, if he be constant to do My commandments and My judgments, as at this day. (1 Chronicles 28:7)
79	**An Uncommon Enemy Will Require Uncommon Wisdom.**	**MARCH 20** / *1 Samuel 21-23* And the Lord was with Jehoshaphat, because he walked in the first ways of his father David, and sought not unto Baalim; Therefore the Lord stablished the kingdom in his hand; and all Judah brought to Jehoshaphat presents; and he had riches and honour in abundance. (2 Chronicles 17:3,5)
80	**What You Say Is Not As Important As What Others Remember.**	**MARCH 21** / *1 Samuel 24-26* And they rose early in the morning, and went forth into the wilderness of Tekoa: and as they went forth, Jehoshaphat stood and said, Hear me, O Judah, and ye inhabitants of Jerusalem; Believe in the Lord your God, so shall ye be established; believe His prophets, so shall ye prosper. (2 Chronicles 20:20)
81	**Never Discuss Your Problem With Someone Incapable Of Solving It.**	**MARCH 22** / *1 Samuel 27-31* Go, enquire of the Lord for me, and for them that are left in Israel and in Judah, concerning the words of the book that is found: for great is the wrath of the Lord that is poured out upon us, because our fathers have not kept the word of the Lord, to do after all that is written in this book. (2 Chronicles 34:21)
82	**Joy Is The Divine Reward For Discerning The Divine Purpose Of The Immediate Moment.**	**MARCH 23** / *2 Samuel 1-3* But they mocked the messengers of God, and despised His words, and misused His prophets, until the wrath of the Lord arose against His people, till there was no remedy. (2 Chronicles 36:16)
83	**God Never Responds To Pain, But He Always Responds To Pursuit.**	**MARCH 24** / *2 Samuel 4-6* For Ezra had prepared his heart to seek the law of the Lord, and to do it, and to teach in Israel statutes and judgments. (Ezra 7:10)
84	**When You Get Involved With God's Dream, He Will Get Involved With Your Dream.**	**MARCH 25** / *2 Samuel 7-9* And thou, Ezra, after the wisdom of thy God, that is in thine hand, set magistrates and judges, which may judge all the people that are beyond the river, all such as know the laws of thy God; and teach ye them that know them not. (Ezra 7:25)

WISDOM KEYS OF
MIKE MURDOCK©

WISDOM KEY#	WISDOM KEY	MEMORY SCRIPTURES ON THE WORD OF GOD
85	The True Function Of Wisdom Is Order.	**MARCH 26 /** *2 Samuel 10-12* But if ye turn unto Me, and keep My commandments, and do them; though there were of you cast out unto the uttermost part of the heaven, yet will I gather them from thence, and will bring them unto the place that I have chosen to set My name there. (Nehemiah 1:9)
86	Confrontation Is The Attempt To Preserve A Relationship.	**MARCH 27 /** *2 Samuel 13-15* Receive, I pray thee, the law from His mouth, and lay up His words in thine heart. (Job 22:22)
87	The Wise Never Discuss What They Want Others To Forget.	**MARCH 28 /** *2 Samuel 16-18* Neither have I gone back from the commandment of His lips; I have esteemed the words of His mouth more than my necessary food. (Job 23:12)
88	The Proof Of Love Is The Passion To Pleasure.	**MARCH 29 /** *2 Samuel 19-23* But his delight is in the law of the Lord; and in His law doth he meditate day and night. (Psalm 1:2)
89	Pain Is The Proof Of Disorder.	**MARCH 30 /** *2 Samuel 24 - 1 Kings 2* But his delight is in the law of the Lord; and in His law doth he meditate day and night. And he shall be like a tree planted by the rivers of water, that bringeth forth his fruit in his season; his leaf also shall not wither; and whatsoever he doeth shall prosper. (Psalm 1:2,3)
90	Debt Is The Proof Of Greed.	**MARCH 31 /** *1 Kings 3-5* The words of the Lord are pure words: as silver tried in a furnace of earth, purified seven times. (Psalm 12:6)
91	Giving Is The Only Proof You Have Conquered Greed.	**APRIL 1 /** *1 Kings 6-8* For I have kept the ways of the Lord, and have not wickedly departed from my God. For all His judgments were before me, and I did not put away His statutes from me. (Psalm 18:21,22)

WISDOM KEYS OF
MIKE MURDOCK©

WISDOM KEY#	WISDOM KEY	MEMORY SCRIPTURES ON THE WORD OF GOD
92	If Time Heals, God Is Unnecessary.	**APRIL 2 /** *1 Kings 9-11* As for God, His way is perfect: the word of the Lord is tried: He is a buckler to all those that trust in Him. (Psalm 18:30)
93	Loneliness Is Not The Absence Of Affection But The Absence Of Direction.	**APRIL 3 /** *1 Kings 12-14* The law of the Lord is perfect, converting the soul: the testimony of the Lord is sure, making wise the simple. (Psalm 19:7)
94	Money Is Merely A Reward For Solving Problems.	**APRIL 4 /** *1 Kings 15-17* The statutes of the Lord are right, rejoicing the heart: the commandment of the Lord is pure, enlightening the eyes. (Psalm 19:8)
95	Access Becomes A Continuous Test.	**APRIL 5 /** *1 Kings 18-22* Moreover by them is thy servant warned: and in keeping of them there is great reward. (Psalm 19:11)
96	When Fatigue Walks In, Faith Walks Out.	**APRIL 6 /** *2 Kings 1-3* For the word of the Lord is right; and all His works are done in truth. (Psalm 33:4)
97	Patience Is The Weapon That Forces Deception To Reveal Itself.	**APRIL 7 /** *2 Kings 4-6* By the word of the Lord were the heavens made; and all the host of them by the breath of His mouth. (Psalm 33:6)
98	Any Step Toward Self-Sufficiency Is A Step Away From God.	**APRIL 8 /** *2 Kings 7-9* The law of his God is in his heart; none of his steps shall slide. (Psalm 37:31)

WISDOM KEYS OF
MIKE MURDOCK©

WISDOM KEY#	WISDOM KEY	MEMORY SCRIPTURES ON THE WORD OF GOD
99	Ignorance Is The Only Weapon Satan Can Effectively Use Against You.	**APRIL 9** / *2 Kings 10-12* I delight to do Thy will, O my God: yea, Thy law is within my heart. (Psalm 40:8)
100	A Tired Mind Rarely Makes Good Decisions.	**APRIL 10** / *2 Kings 13-15* The Lord gave the word: great was the company of those that published it. (Psalm 68:11)
101	An Uncommon Dream Requires Uncommon Patience.	**APRIL 11** / *2 Kings 16-18* Give ear, O My people, to My law: incline your ears to the words of My mouth. (Psalm 78:1)
102	Anything You Do Not Have Is Stored In Someone Near You, And Love Is The Secret Map To The Treasure.	**APRIL 12** / *2 Kings 19-23* If his children forsake My law, and walk not in My judgments; If they break My statutes, and keep not My commandments; Then will I visit their transgression with the rod, and their iniquity with stripes. (Psalm 89:30-32)
103	The Proof Of Mediocrity Is The Resentment Of Excellence.	**APRIL 13** / *2 Kings 24 - 1 Chronicles 1* Blessed is the man whom Thou chastenest, O Lord, and teachest him out of Thy law; (Psalm 94:12)
104	Conduct Permitted Is Conduct Taught.	**APRIL 14** / *1 Chronicles 2-4* Bless the Lord, ye His angels, that excel in strength, that do His commandments, hearkening unto the voice of His word. (Psalm 103:20)
105	A Seed Of Nothing Always Creates A Season Of Nothing.	**APRIL 15** / *1 Chronicles 5-7* He hath remembered His covenant for ever, the word which He commanded to a thousand generations. (Psalm 105:8)

WISDOM KEYS OF
MIKE MURDOCK ©

WISDOM KEY#	WISDOM KEY	MEMORY SCRIPTURES ON THE WORD OF GOD
106	**Mentorship Is Wisdom Without The Pain.**	**APRIL 16 /** *1 Chronicles 8-10* Until the time that His word came: the word of the Lord tried him. (Psalm 105:19)
107	**An Unconquered Weakness Always Births A Tragedy.**	**APRIL 17 /** *1 Chronicles 11-13* He sent His word, and healed them, and delivered them from their destructions. (Psalm 107:20)
108	**Anger Is Simply Passion Requiring An Appropriate Focus.**	**APRIL 18 /** *1 Chronicles 14-16* The works of His hands are verity and judgment; all His commandments are sure. (Psalm 111:7)
109	**Bitterness Is Deadlier Than Betrayal.**	**APRIL 19 /** *1 Chronicles 17-21* Blessed are the undefiled in the way, who walk in the law of the Lord. (Psalm 119:1)
110	**An Uncommon Assignment Attracts An Uncommon Adversary.**	**APRIL 20 /** *1 Chronicles 22-24* Thou hast commanded us to keep Thy precepts diligently. (Psalm 119:4)
111	**Gifts Reveal The Character Of Those Who Receive Them.**	**APRIL 21 /** *1 Chronicles 25-27* O that my ways were directed to keep Thy statutes! (Psalm 119:5)
112	**Giving Is Emptying Your Present To Fill Up Your Future.**	**APRIL 22 /** *1 Chronicles 28 - 2 Chronicles 1* Then shall I not be ashamed, when I have respect unto all Thy commandments. (Psalm 119:6)

WISDOM KEYS OF
MIKE MURDOCK©

WISDOM KEY#	WISDOM KEY	MEMORY SCRIPTURES ON THE WORD OF GOD
113	Obedience Is The Only Thing God Has Ever Required Of Man.	**APRIL 23** / *2 Chronicles 2-4* I will praise Thee with uprightness of heart, when I shall have learned Thy righteous judgments. (Psalm 119:7)
114	Business Is Simply Solving A Problem For An Agreed Reward.	**APRIL 24** / *2 Chronicles 5-7* I will keep Thy statutes: O forsake me not utterly. (Psalm 119:8)
115	Currents Of Favor Begin To Flow The Moment That You Solve A Problem For Someone.	**APRIL 25** / *2 Chronicles 8-10* Wherewithal shall a young man cleanse his way? by taking heed thereto according to Thy word. (Psalm 119:9)
116	Champions Are Willing To Walk Away From Something They Desire To Protect Something Else They Love.	**APRIL 26** / *2 Chronicles 11-15* Thy word have I hid in mine heart, that I might not sin against Thee. (Psalm 119:11)
117	An Uncontested Enemy Will Flourish.	**APRIL 27** / *2 Chronicles 16-18* Blessed art Thou, O Lord: teach me Thy statutes. (Psalm 119:12)
118	God Creates Seasons; Discoveries Schedule Them.	**APRIL 28** / *2 Chronicles 19-21* With my lips have I declared all the judgments of thy mouth. (Psalm 119:13)
119	God Had A Son But He Wanted A Family; He Sowed His Son To Create His Family.	**APRIL 29** / *2 Chronicles 22-24* I have rejoiced in the way of Thy testimonies, as much as in all riches. (Psalm 119:14)

WISDOM KEYS OF
MIKE MURDOCK©

WISDOM KEY#	WISDOM KEY	MEMORY SCRIPTURES ON THE WORD OF GOD
120	**God Sent His Son, But He Left His Book.**	**APRIL 30 /** *2 Chronicles 25-27* I will meditate in Thy precepts, and have respect unto Thy ways. (Psalm 119:15)
121	**Champions Are Willing To Do Things They Hate To Create Something Else They Love.**	**MAY 1 /** *2 Chronicles 28-30* I will delight myself in Thy statutes: I will not forget Thy word. (Psalm 119:16)
122	**Everything God Created Is A Solution To A Problem.**	**MAY 2 /** *2 Chronicles 31-33* Deal bountifully with Thy servant, that I may live, and keep Thy word. (Psalm 119:17)
123	**Every Friendship Nurtures A Strength Or A Weakness.**	**MAY 3 /** *2 Chronicles 34 - Ezra 2* Open Thou mine eyes, that I may behold wondrous things out of Thy law. (Psalm 119:18)
124	**Bad Times Bring Good People Together.**	**MAY 4 /** *Ezra 3-5* Princes also did sit and speak against me: but Thy servant did meditate in Thy statutes. (Psalm 119:23)
125	**One Day Of Doubt Will Create 365 Days Of Pain.**	**MAY 5 /** *Ezra 6-8* My soul cleaveth unto the dust: quicken Thou me according to Thy word. (Psalm 119:25)
126	**God Will Never Ask For Something You Don't Have; He Will Always Ask For Something You Want To Keep.**	**MAY 6 /** *Ezra 9 - Nehemiah 1* I have declared my ways, and Thou heardest me: teach me Thy statutes. (Psalm 119:26)

WISDOM KEYS OF
MIKE MURDOCK©

WISDOM KEY#	WISDOM KEY	MEMORY SCRIPTURES ON THE WORD OF GOD
127	Order Is God's Only Obsession.	**MAY 7** / *Nehemiah 2-4* Make me to understand the way of Thy precepts: so shall I talk of Thy wondrous works. (Psalm 119:27)
128	Creativity Is The Search For Options; Focus Is The Elimination Of Them.	**MAY 8** / *Nehemiah 5-7* My soul melteth for heaviness: strengthen Thou me according unto Thy word. (Psalm 119:28)
129	If You Don't Know Where You Belong, You Will Adapt To Where You Are.	**MAY 9** / *Nehemiah 8-10* Remove from me the way of lying: and grant me Thy law graciously. (Psalm 119:29)
130	Give Another What He Cannot Find Anywhere Else And He Will Keep Returning.	**MAY 10** / *Nehemiah 11 - Esther 2* Teach me, O Lord, the way of Thy statutes; and I shall keep it unto the end. (Psalm 119:33)
131	Endurance Demoralizes Your Adversary.	**MAY 11** / *Esther 3-5* Give me understanding, and I shall keep Thy law; yea, I shall observe it with my whole heart. (Psalm 119:34)
132	Miracles Do Not Go Where They Are Needed; They Go Where They Are Expected.	**MAY 12** / *Esther 6-8* Stablish Thy word unto Thy servant, who is devoted to Thy fear. (Psalm 119:38)
133	If What You Hold In Your Hand Is Not Enough To Be Your Harvest, It Must Be Your Seed.	**MAY 13** / *Esther 9 - Job 1* Behold, I have longed after Thy precepts: quicken me in Thy righteousness. (Psalm 119:40)

WISDOM KEYS OF
MIKE MURDOCK©

WISDOM KEY#	WISDOM KEY	MEMORY SCRIPTURES ON THE WORD OF GOD
134	**Access Creates Demands; Demands Create Expectations; Expectations Create Distraction; Distraction Creates Failure.**	**MAY 14 /** *Job 2-4* So shall I have wherewith to answer him that reproacheth me: for I trust in Thy word. (Psalm 119:42)
135	**Debt Is Emptying Your Future To Fill Up Your Present.**	**MAY 15 /** *Job 5-7* So shall I keep Thy law continually for ever and ever. (Psalm 119:44)
136	**Provision Is Only Guaranteed At The Place Of Your Assignment.**	**MAY 16 /** *Job 8-10* And I will walk at liberty: for I seek Thy precepts. (Psalm 119:45)
137	**God Disguises His Greatest Gifts In The Most Flawed Vessels So Only The Most Passionate Qualify To Release Them.**	**MAY 17 /** *Job 11-15* And I will delight myself in Thy commandments, which I have loved. (Psalm 119:47)
138	**Losers Focus On What They Are Going Through; Champions Focus On What They Are Going To.**	**MAY 18 /** *Job 16-18* My hands also will I lift up unto Thy commandments, which I have loved; and I will meditate in Thy statutes. (Psalm 119:48)
139	**Silence Cannot Be Misquoted.**	**MAY 19 /** *Job 19-21* Remember the word unto Thy servant, upon which thou hast caused me to hope. (Psalm 119:49)
140	**Money Does Not Change You; It Magnifies What You Already Are.**	**MAY 20 /** *Job 22-24* This is my comfort in my affliction: for Thy word hath quickened me. (Psalm 119:50)

WISDOM KEYS OF MIKE MURDOCK©

WISDOM KEY#	WISDOM KEY	MEMORY SCRIPTURES ON THE WORD OF GOD
141	The Holy Spirit Is The Only Person Capable Of Being Completely Satisfied With You.	**MAY 21** / *Job 25-27* Thy statutes have been my songs in the house of my pilgrimage. (Psalm 119:54)
142	Diligence Is Immediate Attention To An Assigned Task.	**MAY 22** / *Job 28-30* I am a companion of all them that fear Thee, and of them that keep Thy precepts. (Psalm 119:63)
143	Restlessness Is Your Future Whimpering At Your Feet Begging For Instruction.	**MAY 23** / *Job 31-33* Thou hast dealt well with Thy servant, O Lord, according unto Thy word. (Psalm 119:65)
144	God Will Never Authorize A Man To Marry A Woman Who Refuses To Follow, Nor A Woman To Marry A Man Who Refuses To Lead.	**MAY 24** / *Job 34-38* Before I was afflicted I went astray: but now have I kept Thy word. (Psalm 119:67)
145	Men Do Not Drown By Falling In The Water; They Drown By Staying There.	**MAY 25** / *Job 39-41* It is good for me that I have been afflicted; that I might learn Thy statutes. (Psalm 119:71)
146	The Purpose Of Memory Is To Revisit Places Of Pleasure.	**MAY 26** / *Job 42 - Psalms 2* The law of Thy mouth is better unto me than thousands of gold and silver. (Psalm 119:72)
147	Nothing Leaves Heaven Until Something Leaves Earth.	**MAY 27** / *Psalms 3-5* Let my heart be sound in Thy statutes; that I be not ashamed. (Psalm 119:80)

WISDOM KEYS OF
MIKE MURDOCK ©

WISDOM KEY#	WISDOM KEY	MEMORY SCRIPTURES ON THE WORD OF GOD
148	The Holy Spirit Is The Only Person You Are Required To Obey.	**MAY 28 /** *Psalms 6-8* My soul fainteth for Thy salvation: but I hope in Thy word. (Psalm 119:81)
149	Failure Is Not An Event, But Merely An Opinion.	**MAY 29 /** *Psalms 9-11* For ever, O Lord, Thy word is settled in heaven. (Psalm 119:89)
150	Stop Looking At Where You Have Been And Start Looking At Where You Can Be.	**MAY 30 /** *Psalms 12-14* Unless Thy law had been my delights, I should then have perished in mine affliction. (Psalm 119:92)
151	What You Say Determines What God Is Willing To Do For You.	**MAY 31 /** *Psalms 15-19* I will never forget Thy precepts: for with them Thou hast quickened me. (Psalm 119:93)
152	Pain Is Not Your Enemy—Merely The Proof That You Have One.	**JUNE 1 /** *Psalms 20-22* O how love I Thy law! it is my meditation all the day. (Psalm 119:97)
153	Flattery Is Speaking Good Words For Wrong Reasons.	**JUNE 2 /** *Psalms 23-25* I understand more than the ancients, because I keep Thy precepts. (Psalm 119:100)
154	Only A Fool Negotiates With A Giver.	**JUNE 3 /** *Psalms 26-28* I have refrained my feet from every evil way, that I might keep Thy word. (Psalm 119:101)

WISDOM KEYS OF
MIKE MURDOCK©

WISDOM KEY#	WISDOM KEY	MEMORY SCRIPTURES ON THE WORD OF GOD
155	The Person Of Jesus Creates Your Peace; The Principles Of Jesus Create Your Prosperity.	**JUNE 4 /** *Psalms 29-31* How sweet are Thy words unto my taste! yea, sweeter than honey to my mouth! (Psalm 119:103)
156	Fame Will Birth Pursuit; Pursuit Will Birth Demands; Demands Will Birth Distractions; Distractions Will Birth Failure.	**JUNE 5 /** *Psalms 32-34* Through Thy precepts I get understanding: therefore I hate every false way. (Psalm 119:104)
157	The Only Reason Men Fail Is Broken Focus.	**JUNE 6 /** *Psalms 35-37* Thy word is a lamp unto my feet, and a light unto my path. (Psalm 119:105)
158	Jealousy Is Believing Another Received What You Deserved.	**JUNE 7 /** *Psalms 38-42* Thy testimonies have I taken as an heritage for ever: for they are the rejoicing of my heart. (Psalm 119:111)
159	The Waves Of Yesterday's Disobedience Will Splash On The Shores Of Tomorrow For A Season.	**JUNE 8 /** *Psalms 43-45* Thou art my hiding place and my shield: I hope in Thy word. (Psalm 119:114)
160	The Quality Of A Nation Is Revealed By The Quality Of The Leader God Permits To Govern Them.	**JUNE 9 /** *Psalms 46-48* Hold Thou me up, and I shall be safe: and I will have respect unto Thy statutes continually. (Psalm 119:117)
161	Something You Already Have Can Create Anything Else You Will Ever Want.	**JUNE 10 /** *Psalms 49-51* Thou hast trodden down all them that err from Thy statutes: for their deceit is falsehood. (Psalm 119:118)

WISDOM KEYS OF
MIKE MURDOCK©

WISDOM KEY#	WISDOM KEY	MEMORY SCRIPTURES ON THE WORD OF GOD
162	**The Presence Of God Is The Only Place Your Weakness Will Die.**	*JUNE 11 / Psalms 52-54* Deal with Thy servant according unto Thy mercy, and teach me Thy statutes. (Psalm 119:124)
163	**Focus Creates Blindness.**	*JUNE 12 / Psalms 55-57* Therefore I love thy commandments above gold; yea, above fine gold. (Psalm 119:127)
164	**The Pain Of Your Past Will Decide Your Passion For The Future.**	*JUNE 13 / Psalms 58-60* Therefore I esteem all Thy precepts concerning all things to be right; and I hate every false way. (Psalm 119:128)
165	**Nobody Is Ever As They First Appear.**	*JUNE 14 / Psalms 61-65* The entrance of Thy words giveth light; it giveth understanding unto the simple. (Psalm 119:130)
166	**Satan Always Attacks Those Next In Line For A Promotion.**	*JUNE 15 / Psalms 66-68* Order my steps in Thy word: and let not any iniquity have dominion over me. (Psalm 119:133)
167	**The Quickest Cure For Ingratitude Is Loss.**	*JUNE 16 / Psalms 69-71* Thy word is very pure: therefore Thy servant loveth it. (Psalm 119:140)
168	**The Anointing You Respect Is The Anointing That Increases In Your Life.**	*JUNE 17 / Psalms 72-74* Thy righteousness is an everlasting righteousness, and Thy law is the truth. (Psalm 119:142)

WISDOM KEYS OF MIKE MURDOCK©

WISDOM KEY#	WISDOM KEY	MEMORY SCRIPTURES ON THE WORD OF GOD
169	The Price God Was Willing To Pay Reveals The Worth Of The Product He Saw.	**JUNE 18** / *Psalms 75-77* Mine eyes prevent the night watches, that I might meditate in thy word. (Psalm 119:148)
170	The Seed Forces The Soil To Expose Its True Character.	**JUNE 19** / *Psalms 78-80* Plead my cause, and deliver me: quicken me according to Thy word. (Psalm 119:154)
171	The Problem Closest To You Is Your Door Out Of Trouble.	**JUNE 20** / *Psalms 81-83* Salvation is far from the wicked: for they seek not Thy statutes. (Psalm 119:155)
172	Parasites View Your Weakness As A Reason To Leave; Protégés View Your Weakness As A Reason To Stay.	**JUNE 21** / *Psalms 84-88* Thy word is true from the beginning: and every one of Thy righteous judgments endureth for ever. (Psalm 119:160)
173	Satan's Favorite Entry Point Into Your Life Is Always Through Someone Close To You.	**JUNE 22** / *Psalms 89-91* I rejoice at Thy word, as one that findeth great spoil. (Psalm 119:162)
174	The Ungodly Give Gifts To Influence Decisions; The Godly Give Gifts To Prove Love.	**JUNE 23** / *Psalms 92-94* I hate and abhor lying: but Thy law do I love. (Psalm 119:163)
175	The Difference Between Seasons Is Simply An Instruction.	**JUNE 24** / *Psalms 95-97* Great peace have they which love Thy law: and nothing shall offend them. (Psalm 119:165)

WISDOM KEYS OF
MIKE MURDOCK©

WISDOM KEY#	WISDOM KEY	MEMORY SCRIPTURES ON THE WORD OF GOD
176	**The Price Of God's Presence Is Time.**	*JUNE 25 / Psalms 98-100* My lips shall utter praise, when Thou hast taught me Thy statutes. (Psalm 119:171)
177	**Information Births Confidence.**	*JUNE 26 / Psalms 101-103* My tongue shall speak of Thy word: for all Thy commandments are righteousness. (Psalm 119:172)
178	**The Problem You Are Willing To Solve Determines Who Pursues You.**	*JUNE 27 / Psalms 104-106* If thy children will keep My covenant and My testimony that I shall teach them, their children shall also sit upon Thy throne for evermore. (Psalm 132:12)
179	**Parasites Want What You Have Earned; Protégés Want What You Have Learned.**	*JUNE 28 / Psalms 107-111* Fire, and hail; snow, and vapour; stormy wind fulfilling His word. (Psalm 148:8)
180	**Struggle Is The Proof That You Have Not Yet Been Conquered.**	*JUNE 29 / Psalms 112-114* My son, forget not My law; but let thine heart keep My commandments: For length of days, and long life, and peace, shall they add to thee. (Proverbs 3:1,2)
181	**Those Without Your Memories Cannot Feel Your Pain.**	*JUNE 30 / Psalms 115-117* Happy is the man that findeth wisdom, and the man that getteth understanding. She is more precious than rubies: and all the things thou canst desire are not to be compared unto her. (Proverbs 3:13,15)
182	**Your Seed Will Expose The Character Of The Soil.**	*JULY 1 / Psalms 118-120* Let thine heart retain My words: keep My commandments, and live. (Proverbs 4:4)

WISDOM KEYS OF
MIKE MURDOCK©

WISDOM KEY#	WISDOM KEY	MEMORY SCRIPTURES ON THE WORD OF GOD
183	The Three Rewards For Christ Are Forgiveness, A Friend And A Future.	**JULY 2** / *Psalms 121-123* Get wisdom, get understanding: forget it not; neither decline from the words of my mouth. Forsake her not, and she shall preserve thee: love her, and she shall keep thee. (Proverbs 4:5,6)
184	Integrity Cannot Be Proven, Only Discerned.	**JULY 3** / *Psalms 124-126* Wisdom is the principal thing; therefore get wisdom: and with all thy getting get understanding. Exalt her, and she shall promote thee: she shall bring thee to honour, when thou dost embrace her. (Proverbs 4:7,8)
185	The Problems You Solve Determine The Rewards You Receive.	**JULY 4** / *Psalms 127-129* My son, attend to My words; incline thine ear unto My sayings. Let them not depart from thine eyes; keep them in the midst of thine heart. For they are life unto those that find them, and health to all their flesh. (Proverbs 4:20-22)
186	People Don't Always Remember What You Say; They Always Remember How They Felt When You Said It.	**JULY 5** / *Psalms 130-134* For the commandment is a lamp; and the law is light; and reproofs of instruction are the way of life. (Proverbs 6:23)
187	The Goal Of An Enemy Is To Change Your Self-Portrait.	**JULY 6** / *Psalms 135-137* Keep My commandments, and live; and my law as the apple of thine eye. Bind them upon thy fingers, write them upon the table of thine heart. (Proverbs 7:2,3)
188	Time Will Expose What Interrogation Cannot.	**JULY 7** / *Psalms 138-140* Whoso keepeth the law is a wise son: but he that is a companion of riotous men shameth his father. (Proverbs 28:7)
189	The Quality Of The Soil Determines The Future Of The Seed.	**JULY 8** / *Psalms 141-143* Where there is no vision, the people perish: but he that keepeth the law, happy is he. (Proverbs 29:18)

WISDOM KEYS OF
MIKE MURDOCK ©

WISDOM KEY#	WISDOM KEY	MEMORY SCRIPTURES ON THE WORD OF GOD
190	The Will Of God Is An Attitude—Not A Place.	**JULY 9 /** *Psalms 144-146* Every word of God is pure: He is a shield unto them that put their trust in Him. (Proverbs 30:5)
191	Make Your Future So Big Yesterday Disappears.	**JULY 10 /** *Psalms 147-149* Add thou not unto His words, lest He reprove thee, and thou be found a liar. (Proverbs 30:6)
192	The Quality Of Your Questions Will Determine The Quality Of Your Discoveries.	**JULY 11 /** *Psalms 150 - Proverbs 2* That this is a rebellious people, lying children, children that will not hear the law of the Lord. (Isaiah 30:9)
193	Popularity Is When People Like You; Happiness Is When You Like You.	**JULY 12 /** *Proverbs 3-7* Seek ye out of the book of the Lord, and read: no one of these shall fail, none shall want her mate: for my mouth it hath commanded, and His spirit it hath gathered them. (Isaiah 34:16)
194	True Friends Have The Same Enemies.	**JULY 13 /** *Proverbs 8-10* The grass withereth, the flower fadeth: but the word of our God shall stand for ever. (Isaiah 40:8)
195	To Love Something Is To Find It Desirable; To Respect Something Is To Find It Valuable.	**JULY 14 /** *Proverbs 11-13* The Lord is well pleased for His righteousness` sake; He will magnify the law, and make it honourable. (Isaiah 42:21)
196	The Quality Of Your Seed Determines The Quality Of Your Harvest.	**JULY 15 /** *Proverbs 14-16* O that thou hadst hearkened to My commandments! then had thy peace been as a river, and thy righteousness as the waves of the sea. (Isaiah 48:18)

WISDOM KEYS OF
MIKE MURDOCK ©

WISDOM KEY#	WISDOM KEY	MEMORY SCRIPTURES ON THE WORD OF GOD
197	**The Workings Of God Are Never Proportionate To Your Need Of Him But Proportionate To Your Knowledge Of Him.**	**JULY 16** / *Proverbs 17-19* And I have put My words in thy mouth, and I have covered thee in the shadow of Mine hand, that I may plant the heavens, and lay the foundations of the earth, and say unto Zion, Thou art My people. (Isaiah 51:16)
198	**May You Never Have Anything God Is Unwilling To Give.**	**JULY 17** / *Proverbs 20-22* So shall My word be that goeth forth out of My mouth: it shall not return unto Me void, but it shall accomplish that which I please, and it shall prosper in the thing whereto I sent it. (Isaiah 55:11)
199	**The Season For Research Is Not The Season For Marketing.**	**JULY 18** / *Proverbs 23-25* As for Me, this is My covenant with them, saith the Lord; My spirit that is upon thee, and My words which I have put in thy mouth, shall not depart out of thy mouth, nor out of the mouth of thy seed, nor out of the mouth of thy seed`s seed, saith the Lord, from henceforth and for ever. (Isaiah 59:21)
200	**Someone In Trouble Is Always Your Door Out Of Trouble.**	**JULY 19** / *Proverbs 26-30* Then said the Lord unto me, Thou hast well seen: for I will hasten My word to perform it. (Jeremiah 1:12)
201	**Warfare Is The Proof Your Enemy Has Just Discerned Your Future.**	**JULY 20** / *Proverbs 31 - Ecclesiastes 2* Wherefore thus saith the Lord God of hosts, Because ye speak this word, behold, I will make My words in thy mouth fire, and this people wood, and it shall devour them. (Jeremiah 5:14)
202	**What You Hear Determines What You Become Willing To Change.**	**JULY 21** / *Ecclesiastes 3-5* But this thing commanded I them, saying, Obey My voice, and I will be your God, and ye shall be My people: and walk ye in all the ways that I have commanded you, that it may be well unto you. (Jeremiah 7:23)
203	**The Seed That Leaves Your Hand Never Leaves Your Life; It Enters Your Future Where It Multiplies.**	**JULY 22** / *Ecclesiastes 6-8* The wise men are ashamed, they are dismayed and taken: lo, they have rejected the word of the Lord; and what wisdom is in them? (Jeremiah 8:9)

WISDOM KEYS OF
MIKE MURDOCK©

WISDOM KEY#	WISDOM KEY	MEMORY SCRIPTURES ON THE WORD OF GOD
204	There Are Two Ways To Increase Wisdom: Mistakes And Mentors.	**JULY 23** / *Ecclesiastes 9-11* Thy words were found, and I did eat them; and Thy word was unto me the joy and rejoicing of mine heart: for I am called by Thy name, O Lord God of hosts. (Jeremiah 15:16)
205	Tired Eyes Rarely See A Good Future.	**JULY 24** / *Ecclesiastes 12-Song of Solomon 2* Then I said, I will not make mention of Him, nor speak any more in His name. But His word was in mine heart as a burning fire shut up in my bones, and I was weary with forbearing, and I could not stay. (Jeremiah 20:9)
206	Those Comfortable With Your Weakness May Be Adversarial Toward Your Assignment.	**JULY 25** / *Song of Solomon 3-5* O earth, earth, earth, hear the word of the Lord. (Jeremiah 22:29)
207	Someone Is Always Observing You Who Is Capable Of Greatly Blessing You.	**JULY 26** / *Song of Solomon 6 - Isaiah 2* But if they had stood in My counsel, and had caused My people to hear My words, then they should have turned them from their evil way, and from the evil of their doings. (Jeremiah 23:22)
208	What You Cannot Hate—You Cannot Conquer.	**JULY 27** / *Isaiah 3-5* The prophet that hath a dream, let him tell a dream; and he that hath My word, let him speak My word faithfully. What is the chaff to the wheat? saith the Lord. (Jeremiah 23:28)
209	Whatever You Are Attempting To Live Without Is Something You Do Not Yet Truly Value.	**JULY 28** / *Isaiah 6-8* Is not My word like as a fire? saith the Lord; and like a hammer that breaketh the rock in pieces? (Jeremiah 23:29)
210	Tithe Is Not The Payment Of A Debt—But The Acknowledgement Of It.	**JULY 29** / *Isaiah 9-11* How long shall this be in the heart of the prophets that prophesy lies? yea, they are prophets of the deceit of their own heart. (Jeremiah 23:26)

WISDOM KEYS OF
MIKE MURDOCK©

WISDOM KEY#	WISDOM KEY	MEMORY SCRIPTURES ON THE WORD OF GOD
211	Uncommon Obedience Unleashes Uncommon Favor.	**JULY 30** / *Isaiah 12-14* Therefore now amend your ways and your doings, and obey the voice of the Lord your God; and the Lord will repent him of the evil that he hath pronounced against you. (Jeremiah 26:13)
212	Never Complain About Your Present—If You Are Unwilling To Walk Toward Your Future.	**JULY 31** / *Isaiah 15-17* But this shall be the covenant that I will make with the house of Israel; After those days, saith the Lord, I will put My law in their inward parts, and write it in their hearts; and will be their God, and they shall be My people. (Jeremiah 31:33)
213	Those Who Ask The Questions Determine The Quality Of The Conversation.	**AUGUST 1** / *Isaiah 18-20* Then it shall come to pass, that the sword, which ye feared, shall overtake you there in the land of Egypt, and the famine, whereof ye were afraid, shall follow close after you there in Egypt; and there ye shall die. (Jeremiah 42:16)
214	Submission Cannot Begin Until Agreement Ends.	**AUGUST 2** / *Isaiah 21-25* They are not humbled even unto this day, neither have they feared, nor walked in My law, nor in My statutes, that I set before you and before your fathers. Therefore thus saith the Lord of hosts, the God of Israel; Behold, I will set my face against you for evil, and to cut off all Judah. (Jeremiah 44:10,11)
215	When Satan Wants To Destroy You, He Puts A Person In Your Life.	**AUGUST 3** / *Isaiah 26-28* Because ye multiplied more than the nations that are round about you, and have not walked in My statutes, neither have kept My judgments, neither have done according to the judgments of the nations that are round about you; I, even I, am against thee, and will execute judgments in the midst of thee in the sight of the nations. (Ezekiel 5:7,8)
216	When You Can Manage A Day, You Can Manage Your Life.	**AUGUST 4** / *Isaiah 29-31* And I will give them one heart, and I will put a new spirit within you; and I will take the stony heart out of their flesh, and will give them an heart of flesh: That they may walk in My statutes, and keep Mine ordinances, and do them: and they shall be My people, and I will be their God. (Ezekiel 11:19,20)
217	Tithe Is The Proof Of Your Obedience; Offering Is Proof Of Your Generosity.	**AUGUST 5** / *Isaiah 32-34* For I am the Lord: I will speak, and the word that I shall speak shall come to pass; it shall be no more prolonged: for in your days, O rebellious house, will I say the word, and will perform it, saith the Lord God. (Ezekiel 12:25)

WISDOM KEYS OF MIKE MURDOCK©

WISDOM KEY#	WISDOM KEY	MEMORY SCRIPTURES ON THE WORD OF GOD
218	What Enters You Determines What Exits You.	**AUGUST 6** / *Isaiah 35-37* Yet say ye, Why? doth not the son bear the iniquity of the father? When the son hath done that which is lawful and right, and hath kept all My statutes, and hath done them, he shall surely live. (Ezekiel 18:19)
219	Nothing Is Ever As Bad As It First Appears.	**AUGUST 7** / *Isaiah 38-40* But if the wicked will turn from all his sins that he hath committed, and keep all My statutes, and do that which is lawful and right, he shall surely live, he shall not die. (Ezekiel 18:21)
220	Those Who Impart Knowledge Are Also Capable Of Imparting Error.	**AUGUST 8** / *Isaiah 41-43* I the Lord have spoken it: it shall come to pass, and I will do it; I will not go back, neither will I spare, neither will I repent; according to thy ways, and according to thy doings, shall they judge thee, saith the Lord God. (Ezekiel 24:14)
221	That Which Becomes Familiar Becomes Hidden.	**AUGUST 9** / *Isaiah 44-48* And I will put My spirit within you, and cause you to walk in My statutes, and ye shall keep My judgments, and do them. (Ezekiel 36:27)
222	When You Ask God For A Promotion, He Will Schedule An Adversary.	**AUGUST 10** / *Isaiah 49-51* My people are destroyed for lack of knowledge: because thou hast rejected knowledge, I will also reject thee, that thou shalt be no priest to me: seeing thou hast forgotten the law of thy God, I will also forget thy children. (Hosea 4:6)
223	When You Replay The Past, You Poison The Present.	**AUGUST 11** / *Isaiah 52-54* Behold, the days come, saith the Lord God, that I will send a famine in the land, not a famine of bread, nor a thirst for water, but of hearing the words of the Lord: And they shall wander from sea to sea, and from the north even to the east, they shall run to and fro to seek the word of the Lord, and shall not find it. (Amos 8:11,12)
224	What You Do First Determines What God Does Second.	**AUGUST 12** / *Isaiah 55-57* Yea, they made their hearts as an adamant stone, lest they should hear the law, and the words which the Lord of hosts hath sent in His spirit by the former prophets: therefore came a great wrath from the Lord of hosts. (Zechariah 7:12)

WISDOM KEYS OF
MIKE MURDOCK ©

WISDOM KEY#	WISDOM KEY	MEMORY SCRIPTURES ON THE WORD OF GOD
225	What Happens In Your Mind Will Happen In Time.	**AUGUST 13 /** *Isaiah 58-60* But He answered and said, It is written, Man shall not live by bread alone, but by every word that proceedeth out of the mouth of God. (Matthew 4:4)
226	Nothing Will Ever Dominate Your Life Unless It Happens Daily.	**AUGUST 14 /** *Isaiah 61-63* Think not that I am come to destroy the law, or the prophets: I am not come to destroy, but to fulfil. (Matthew 5:17)
227	Those Who Unlock Your Compassion Are Those To Whom You Have Been Assigned.	**AUGUST 15 /** *Isaiah 64-66* For verily I say unto you, Till heaven and earth pass, one jot or one tittle shall in no wise pass from the law, till all be fulfilled. (Matthew 5:18)
228	The Kindest Word Is An Unkind Word Unsaid.	**AUGUST 16 /** *Jeremiah 1-5* Whosoever therefore shall break one of these least commandments, and shall teach men so, he shall be called the least in the kingdom of heaven: but whosoever shall do and teach them, the same shall be called great in the kingdom of heaven. (Matthew 5:19)
229	When You Delay A Battle, You Delay Your Rewards.	**AUGUST 17 /** *Jeremiah 6-8* Therefore whosoever heareth these sayings of Mine, and doeth them, I will liken him unto a wise man, which built his house upon a rock: (Matthew 7:24)
230	Yesterday Is In The Tomb, Tomorrow Is In The Womb—The Only Place You Will Ever Be Is Today.	**AUGUST 18 /** *Jeremiah 9-11* The centurion answered and said, Lord, I am not worthy that thou shouldest come under My roof: but speak the word only, and My servant shall be healed. (Matthew 8:8)
231	What You Do Is What You Believe.	**AUGUST 19 /** *Jeremiah 12-14* When the even was come, they brought unto Him many that were possessed with devils: and He cast out the spirits with His word, and healed all that were sick: (Matthew 8:16)

WISDOM KEYS OF
MIKE MURDOCK©

WISDOM KEY#	WISDOM KEY	MEMORY SCRIPTURES ON THE WORD OF GOD
232	What You Do Daily Determines What You Become Permanently.	**AUGUST 20** / *Jeremiah 15-17* When any one heareth the word of the kingdom, and understandeth it not, then cometh the wicked one, and catcheth away that which was sown in his heart. This is he which received seed by the way side. (Matthew 13:19)
233	Package Yourself For Where You Are Going Instead Of Where You Have Been.	**AUGUST 21** / *Jeremiah 18-20* But he that received the seed into stony places, the same is he that heareth the word, and anon with joy receiveth it; Yet hath he not root in himself, but dureth for a while: for when tribulation or persecution ariseth because of the word, by and by he is offended. (Matthew 13:20,21)
234	What Grieves You Is A Clue To Something You Were Assigned To Heal.	**AUGUST 22** / *Jeremiah 21-23* He also that received seed among the thorns is he that heareth the word; and the care of this world, and the deceitfulness of riches, choke the word, and he becometh unfruitful. (Matthew 13:22)
235	The Longevity Of Every Relationship Is Decided By The Willingness To Forgive.	**AUGUST 23** / *Jeremiah 24-28* But he that received seed into the good ground is he that heareth the word, and understandeth it; which also beareth fruit, and bringeth forth, some an hundredfold, some sixty, some thirty. (Matthew 13:23)
236	When You Discover Your Assignment, You Will Discover Your Enemy.	**AUGUST 24** / *Jeremiah 29-31* Jesus answered and said unto them, Ye do err, not knowing the scriptures, nor the power of God. (Matthew 22:29)
237	You Have No Right To Anything You Have Not Pursued.	**AUGUST 25** / *Jeremiah 32-34* Heaven and earth shall pass away, but My words shall not pass away. (Matthew 24:35)
238	Whatever You Have Been Given Is Enough To Create Anything Else You Have Been Promised.	**AUGUST 26** / *Jeremiah 35-37* The sower soweth the word. (Mark 4:14)

WISDOM KEYS OF
MIKE MURDOCK©

WISDOM KEY#	WISDOM KEY	MEMORY SCRIPTURES ON THE WORD OF GOD
239	**What You Hear Determines What You Feel.**	**AUGUST 27** / *Jeremiah 38-40* And these are they by the way side, where the word is sown; but when they have heard, Satan cometh immediately, and taketh away the word that was sown in their hearts. (Mark 4:15)
240	**People See What You Are Before They Hear What You Are.**	**AUGUST 28** / *Jeremiah 41-43* And these are they which are sown among thorns; such as hear the word, And the cares of this world, and the deceitfulness of riches, and the lusts of other things entering in, choke the word, and it becometh unfruitful. (Mark 4:18,19)
241	**What You Hate Reveals What You Were Created To Correct.**	**AUGUST 29** / *Jeremiah 44-46* And these are they which are sown on good ground; such as hear the word, and receive it, and bring forth fruit, some thirtyfold, some sixty, and some an hundred. (Mark 4:20)
242	**The Proof Of Humility Is The Willingness To Reach.**	**AUGUST 30** / *Jeremiah 47-51* And with many such parables spake He the word unto them, as they were able to hear it. (Mark 4:33)
243	**Wrong People Birth Sad Seasons.**	**AUGUST 31** / *Jeremiah 52 - Lamentations 2* And He said unto them, Full well ye reject the commandment of God, that ye may keep your own tradition. (Mark 7:9)
244	**Your Chosen Focus Is The World You Have Created For Yourself.**	**SEPTEMBER 1** / *Lamentations 3-5* Making the word of God of none effect through your tradition, which ye have delivered: and many such like things do ye. (Mark 7:13)
245	**Whatever You Sow Is Your Seed; Whatever You Keep Is Your Harvest.**	**SEPTEMBER 2** / *Ezekiel 1-3* And Jesus answering said unto them, Do ye not therefore err, because ye know not the scriptures, neither the power of God? (Mark 12:24)

WISDOM KEYS OF
MIKE MURDOCK©

WISDOM KEY#	WISDOM KEY	MEMORY SCRIPTURES ON THE WORD OF GOD
246	The Battle Of Life Is For Your Mind; The Battle Of The Mind Is For Focus.	**SEPTEMBER 3 /** *Ezekiel 4-6* And thou shalt love the Lord thy God with all thy heart, and with all thy soul, and with all thy mind, and with all thy strength: this is the first commandment. (Mark 12:30)
247	Protocol Will Take You Further Than Genius.	**SEPTEMBER 4 /** *Ezekiel 7-9* And they went forth, and preached every where, the Lord working with them, and confirming the word with signs following. Amen. (Mark 16:20)
248	What You Love The Most Is A Clue To The Gift You Contain.	**SEPTEMBER 5 /** *Ezekiel 10-12* And they were astonished at His doctrine: for His word was with power. (Luke 4:32)
249	The Proof Of Love Is The Desire To Give.	**SEPTEMBER 6 /** *Ezekiel 13-17* Now the parable is this: The seed is the word of God. (Luke 8:11)
250	Your Assignment Will Always Have An Adversary.	**SEPTEMBER 7 /** *Ezekiel 18-20* Those by the way side are they that hear; then cometh the devil, and taketh away the word out of their hearts, lest they should believe and be saved. (Luke 8:12)
251	What You Hear Determines What You Pursue.	**SEPTEMBER 8 /** *Ezekiel 21-23* They on the rock are they, which, when they hear, receive the word with joy; and these have no root, which for a while believe, and in time of temptation fall away. (Luke 8:13)
252	When God Talks To You About A Seed, He Has A Harvest On His Mind.	**SEPTEMBER 9 /** *Ezekiel 24-26* But that on the good ground are they, which in an honest and good heart, having heard the word, keep it, and bring forth fruit with patience. (Luke 8:15)

WISDOM KEYS OF
MIKE MURDOCK ©

WISDOM KEY#	WISDOM KEY	MEMORY SCRIPTURES ON THE WORD OF GOD
253	When You Ignore God, You Schedule A Tragedy.	*SEPTEMBER 10 / Ezekiel 27-29* And he answered and said unto them, My mother and my brethren are these which hear the word of God, and do it. (Luke 8:21)
254	Successful Men Do Daily What Unsuccessful Men Do Occasionally.	*SEPTEMBER 11 / Ezekiel 30-32* But he said, Yea rather, blessed are they that hear the word of God, and keep it. (Luke 11:28)
255	You Are Never Responsible For The Pain Of Those Who Have Ignored Your Counsel.	*SEPTEMBER 12 / Ezekiel 33-35* And they said one to another, Did not our heart burn within us, while he talked with us by the way, and while he opened to us the scriptures? (Luke 24:32)
256	The Proof Of Love Is The Obsession To Protect.	*SEPTEMBER 13 / Ezekiel 36-40* Then he said unto them, O fools, and slow of heart to believe all that the prophets have spoken. (Luke 24:25)
257	Your Goals Force Every Adversary To Express Their Opposition To You.	*SEPTEMBER 14 / Ezekiel 41-43* In the beginning was the Word, and the Word was with God, and the Word was God. (John 1:1)
258	Fathers Decide What Daughters Remember; Mothers Decide What Sons Believe.	*SEPTEMBER 15 / Ezekiel 44-46* And the Word was made flesh, and dwelt among us, (and we beheld His glory, the glory as of the only begotten of the Father,) full of grace and truth. (John 1:14)
259	When You Ask God For A Harvest, He Will Always Ask You For A Seed.	*SEPTEMBER 16 / Ezekiel 47 - Daniel 1* Verily, verily, I say unto you, He that heareth My word, and believeth on Him that sent Me, hath everlasting life, and shall not come into condemnation; but is passed from death unto life. (John 5:24)

WISDOM KEY#	WISDOM KEY	MEMORY SCRIPTURES ON THE WORD OF GOD
260	Mentorship Is Success Without The Wait.	**SEPTEMBER 17 /** *Daniel 2-4* Search the scriptures; for in them ye think ye have eternal life: and they are they which testify of Me. (John 5:39)
261	The Atmosphere You Create Determines The Future Of Your Weakness.	**SEPTEMBER 18 /** *Daniel 5-7* Then said Pilate unto them, Take ye him, and judge him according to your law. The Jews therefore said unto him, It is not lawful for us to put any man to death. (John 18:31)
262	You Will Only Remember Something You Teach.	**SEPTEMBER 19 /** *Daniel 8-10* I know that ye are Abraham`s seed; but ye seek to kill me, because My word hath no place in you. (John 8:37)
263	The Proof Of Love Is The Willingness To Change.	**SEPTEMBER 20 /** *Daniel 11 - Hosea 3* He that rejecteth Me, and receiveth not My words, hath one that judgeth Him: the word that I have spoken, the same shall judge Him in the last day. (John 12:48)
264	Your Self-Portrait Determines The Kind Of Enemy You Are Willing To Confront.	**SEPTEMBER 21 /** *Hosea 4-6* Now ye are clean through the word which I have spoken unto you. (John 15:3)
265	Where You Are Determines What Dies Within You.	**SEPTEMBER 22 /** *Hosea 7-9* If ye abide in Me, and My words abide in you, ye shall ask what ye will, and it shall be done unto you. (John 15:7)
266	When You Open Your Hands, God Will Open His Windows.	**SEPTEMBER 23 /** *Hosea 10-12* If ye keep My commandments, ye shall abide in My love; even as I have kept My Father`s commandments, and abide in His love. (John 15:10)

WISDOM KEYS OF MIKE MURDOCK©

WISDOM KEY#	WISDOM KEY	MEMORY SCRIPTURES ON THE WORD OF GOD
267	Where You Are Determines What Grows Within You—Your Weakness Or Your Strength.	**SEPTEMBER 24** / *Hosea 13 - Joel 1* These things have I spoken unto you, that My joy might remain in you, and that your joy might be full. (John 15:11)
268	The First Step Toward Success Is The Willingness To Listen.	**SEPTEMBER 25** / *Joel 2 - Amos 1* But we will give ourselves continually to prayer, and to the ministry of the word. (Acts 6:4)
269	You Cannot Be What You Are Not, But You Can Become What You Are Not.	**SEPTEMBER 26** / *Amos 2-4* And the word of God increased; and the number of the disciples multiplied in Jerusalem greatly; and a great company of the priests were obedient to the faith. (Acts 6:7)
270	The Proof Of Love Is The Willingness To Correct.	**SEPTEMBER 27** / *Amos 5-9* Therefore they that were scattered abroad went every where preaching the word. (Acts 8:4)
271	Your Assignment Decides Your Adversity.	**SEPTEMBER 28** / *Obadiah 1 - Jonah 2* But the word of God grew and multiplied. (Acts 12:24)
272	The Proof Of Love Is The Willingness To Listen.	**SEPTEMBER 29** / *Jonah 3 - Micah 1* These were more noble than those in Thessalonica, in that they received the word with all readiness of mind, and searched the scriptures daily, whether those things were so. Therefore many of them believed; (Acts 17:11,12)
273	When You Sow What You Have Been Given, You Will Reap What You Have Been Promised.	**SEPTEMBER 30** / *Micah 2-4* For he mightily convinced the Jews, and that publickly, shewing by the scriptures that Jesus was Christ. (Acts 18:28)

WISDOM KEY#	WISDOM KEY	MEMORY SCRIPTURES ON THE WORD OF GOD
274	Where You Are Determines What You Hear; What You Hear Determines What You Believe.	**OCTOBER 1** / *Micah 5-7* And now, brethren, I commend you to God, and to the word of His grace, which is able to build you up, and to give you an inheritance among all them which are sanctified. (Acts 20:32)
275	The Greatest Success Quality On Earth Is The Willingness To Become.	**OCTOBER 2** / *Nahum 1-3* But this I confess unto thee, that after the way which they call heresy, so worship I the God of my fathers, believing all things which are written in the law and in the prophets. (Acts 24:14)
276	Your Reactions Reveal Your Character.	**OCTOBER 3** / *Habakkuk 1-3* And when they had appointed him a day, there came many to him into his lodging; to whom he expounded and testified the kingdom of God, persuading them concerning Jesus, both out of the law of Moses, and out of the prophets, from morning till evening. And some believed the things which were spoken. (Acts 28:23,24)
277	The Proof Of Loyalty Is The Unwillingness To Betray.	**OCTOBER 4** / *Zephaniah 1 - Haggai 2* For I am not ashamed of the gospel of Christ: for it is the power of God unto salvation to every one that believeth; to the Jew first, and also to the Greek. (Romans 1:16)
278	Your Enemies Decide Your Promotions.	**OCTOBER 5** / *Zechariah 1-3* For not the hearers of the law are just before God, but the doers of the law shall be justified. (Romans 2:13)
279	Your Attitude Determines Your Access.	**OCTOBER 6** / *Zechariah 4-6* Therefore by the deeds of the law there shall no flesh be justified in His sight: for by the law is the knowledge of sin. (Romans 3:20)
280	You Can Create With Your Seed What You Cannot Buy With Your Money.	**OCTOBER 7** / *Zechariah 7-9* He staggered not at the promise of God through unbelief; but was strong in faith, giving glory to God; And being fully persuaded that, what he had promised, he was able also to perform. (Romans 4:20,21)

WISDOM KEY#	WISDOM KEY	MEMORY SCRIPTURES ON THE WORD OF GOD
281	**The Attitude Of The Servant Determines The Atmosphere Of The Palace.**	**OCTOBER 8** / *Zechariah 10-12* Wherefore the law is holy, and the commandment holy, and just, and good. (Romans 7:12)
282	**The Most Dangerous Person In Your Life Is The One Who Feeds Your Doubts.**	**OCTOBER 9** / *Zechariah 13 - Malachi 1* For I delight in the law of God after the inward man. (Romans 7:22)
283	**You Will Never Be Promoted Until You Become Overqualified For Your Present Assignment.**	**OCTOBER 10** / *Malachi 2-4* But what saith it? The word is nigh thee, even in thy mouth, and in thy heart: that is, the word of faith, which we preach. (Romans 10:8)
284	**The Proof Of Order Is The Absence Of Strife.**	**OCTOBER 11** / *Matthew 1-5* So then faith cometh by hearing, and hearing by the word of God. (Romans 10:17)
285	**Crisis Is Simply An Invitation To A Miracle.**	**OCTOBER 12** / *Matthew 6-8* For whatsoever things were written aforetime were written for our learning, that we through patience and comfort of the scriptures might have hope. (Romans 15:4)
286	**Never Gaze At Something That Does Not Belong In Your Future.**	**OCTOBER 13** / *Matthew 9-11* If any man think himself to be a prophet, or spiritual, let him acknowledge that the things that I write unto you are the commandments of the Lord. (1 Corinthians 14:37)
287	**Your Seed Is A Photograph Of Your Faith.**	**OCTOBER 14** / *Matthew 12-14* Where is the wise? where is the scribe? where is the disputer of this world? hath not God made foolish the wisdom of this world? (1 Corinthians 1:20)

WISDOM KEYS OF
MIKE MURDOCK©

WISDOM KEY#	WISDOM KEY	MEMORY SCRIPTURES ON THE WORD OF GOD
288	Where You Are Determines Who Sees You.	**OCTOBER 15** / *Matthew 15-17* For we are not as many, which corrupt the word of God: but as of sincerity, but as of God, in the sight of God speak we in Christ. (2 Corinthians 2:17)
289	The Proof Of Desire Is Pursuit.	**OCTOBER 16** / *Matthew 18-20* Who also hath made us able ministers of the new testament; not of the letter, but of the spirit: for the letter killeth, but the spirit giveth life. (2 Corinthians 3:6)
290	You Will Only Have Significant Success With Something That Is An Obsession.	**OCTOBER 17** / *Matthew 21-23* Having therefore these promises, dearly beloved, let us cleanse ourselves from all filthiness of the flesh and spirit, perfecting holiness in the fear of God. (2 Corinthians 7:1)
291	The Proofs Of Legitimate Authority Are Provision, Protection And Promotion.	**OCTOBER 18** / *Matthew 24-28* But though we, or an angel from heaven, preach any other gospel unto you than that which we have preached unto you, let him be accursed. (Galatians 1:8)
292	Honor Must Become Your Seed Before You Reap It As A Harvest.	**OCTOBER 19** / *Mark 1-3* But I certify you, brethren, that the gospel which was preached of me is not after man. For I neither received it of man, neither was I taught it, but by the revelation of Jesus Christ. (Galatians 1:11,12)
293	Distrust Destroys Passion.	**OCTOBER 20** / *Mark 4-6* Wherefore the law was our schoolmaster to bring us unto Christ, that we might be justified by faith. (Galatians 3:24)
294	Your Seed Is Anything That Benefits Another; Your Harvest Is Anything That Benefits You.	**OCTOBER 21** / *Mark 7-9* For all the law is fulfilled in one word, even in this; Thou shalt love thy neighbour as thyself. (Galatians 5:14)

WISDOM KEYS OF MIKE MURDOCK ©

WISDOM KEY#	WISDOM KEY	MEMORY SCRIPTURES ON THE WORD OF GOD
295	Worship Is The Correction Of Focus.	**OCTOBER 22 /** *Mark 10-12* Bear ye one another's burdens, and so fulfil the law of Christ. (Galatians 6:2)
296	The Pursuit Of The Mentor Reveals The Passion Of The Protégé.	**OCTOBER 23 /** *Mark 13-15* Let him that is taught in the word communicate unto him that teacheth in all good things. (Galatians 6:6)
297	Your Assignment Is Not Your Decision—But Your Discovery.	**OCTOBER 24 /** *Mark 16 - Luke 2* In Whom ye also trusted, after that ye heard the word of truth, the gospel of your salvation: in Whom also after that ye believed, ye were sealed with that holy Spirit of promise. (Ephesians 1:13)
298	Exposure Of Incompetence Usually Births An Adversary.	**OCTOBER 25 /** *Luke 3-7* And take the helmet of salvation, and the sword of the Spirit, which is the word of God. (Ephesians 6:17)
299	The Right Thing At The Wrong Time Becomes The Wrong Thing.	**OCTOBER 26 /** *Luke 8-10* Holding forth the word of life; that I may rejoice in the day of Christ, that I have not run in vain, neither laboured in vain. (Philippians 2:16)
300	Where You Are Matters As Much As What You Are.	**OCTOBER 27 /** *Luke 11-13* Let the word of Christ dwell in you richly in all wisdom; teaching and admonishing one another in psalms and hymns and spiritual songs, singing with grace in your hearts to the Lord. (Colossians 3:16)
301	Your Seed Is The Only Influence You Have Over Your Future.	**OCTOBER 28 /** *Luke 14-16* For this cause also thank we God without ceasing, because, when ye received the word of God which ye heard of us, ye received it not as the word of men, but as it is in truth, the word of God, which effectually worketh also in you that believe. (1 Thessalonians 2:13)

WISDOM KEYS OF
MIKE MURDOCK©

WISDOM KEY#	WISDOM KEY	MEMORY SCRIPTURES ON THE WORD OF GOD
302	Your Understanding Of God Determines Your Message To Men.	**OCTOBER 29** / *Luke 17-19* I charge you by the Lord that this epistle be read unto all the holy brethren. (1 Thessalonians 5:27)
303	The Proof Of Prosperity Is The Ability To Lend; The Proof Of Impatience Is The Willingness To Borrow.	**OCTOBER 30** / *Luke 20-22* Finally, brethren, pray for us, that the word of the Lord may have free course, and be glorified, even as it is with you. (2 Thessalonians 3:1)
304	The Reward Of Submission Is Equal To The Reward Of Agreement.	**OCTOBER 31** / *Luke 23-John 1* And if any man obey not our word by this epistle, note that man, and have no company with him, that he may be ashamed. (2 Thessalonians 3:14)
305	God Gives You A Family To Prepare You For An Enemy.	**NOVEMBER 1** / *John 2-6* Now the end of the commandment is charity out of a pure heart, and of a good conscience, and of faith unfeigned. (1 Timothy 1:5)
306	What You Are Will Outlast What Men Say You Are.	**NOVEMBER 2** / *John 7-9* But we know that the law is good, if a man use it lawfully. (1 Timothy 1:8)
307	The Proof Of Respect Is The Investment Of Time.	**NOVEMBER 3** / *John 10-12* Knowing this, that the law is not made for a righteous man, but for the lawless and disobedient, for the ungodly and for sinners, for unholy and profane, for murderers of fathers and murderers of mothers, for manslayers. (1 Timothy 1:9)
308	Your Tithe Is The Proof Of Your Trust.	**NOVEMBER 4** / *John 13-15* Till I come, give attendance to reading, to exhortation, to doctrine. (1 Timothy 4:13)

WISDOM KEYS OF
MIKE MURDOCK©

WISDOM KEY#	WISDOM KEY	MEMORY SCRIPTURES ON THE WORD OF GOD
309	You Cannot Have A Great Life Unless You Have A Pure Life; You Cannot Have A Pure Life Unless You Have A Pure Mind; You Cannot Have A Pure Mind Unless You Wash It Daily With The Word Of God.	**NOVEMBER 5 /** *John 16-18* Take heed unto thyself, and unto the doctrine; continue in them: for in doing this thou shalt both save thyself, and them that hear thee. (1 Timothy 4:16)
310	Your Belief System Was Chosen For Comfort Or Change.	**NOVEMBER 6 /** *John 19-21* Let the elders that rule well be counted worthy of double honour, especially they who labour in the word and doctrine. (1 Timothy 5:17)
311	The Secret To Knowing A Man Is To Know His Memories.	**NOVEMBER 7 /** *Acts 1-3* Wherein I suffer trouble, as an evil doer, even unto bonds; but the word of God is not bound. (2 Timothy 2:9)
312	Loss Is The First Step Toward Change.	**NOVEMBER 8 /** *Acts 4-8* Study to shew thyself approved unto God, a workman that needeth not to be ashamed, rightly dividing the word of truth. (2 Timothy 2:15)
313	Winners Are Simply Ex-Losers Who Got Mad.	**NOVEMBER 9 /** *Acts 9-11* And that from a child thou hast known the holy scriptures, which are able to make thee wise unto salvation through faith which is in Christ Jesus. (2 Timothy 3:15)
314	The Reward Of Pain Is The Willingness To Listen.	**NOVEMBER 10 /** *Acts 12-14* All scripture is given by inspiration of God, and is profitable for doctrine, for reproof, for correction, for instruction in righteousness: That the man of God may be perfect, throughly furnished unto all good works. (2 Timothy 3:16,17)
315	The Anointing You Sow Into Is The Anointing You Reap From.	**NOVEMBER 11 /** *Acts 15-17* Preach the word; be instant in season, out of season; reprove, rebuke, exhort with all longsuffering and doctrine. (2 Timothy 4:2)

WISDOM KEYS OF
MIKE MURDOCK©

WISDOM KEY#	WISDOM KEY	MEMORY SCRIPTURES ON THE WORD OF GOD
316	**Parasites Want What Is In Your Hand; Protégés Want What Is In Your Heart.**	**NOVEMBER 12** / *Acts 18-20* But hath in due times manifested His word through preaching, which is committed unto me according to the commandment of God our Saviour. (Titus 1:3)
317	**Every Miracle Begins With A Conversation.**	**NOVEMBER 13** / *Acts 21-23* To be discreet, chaste, keepers at home, good, obedient to their own husbands, that the word of God be not blasphemed. (Titus 2:5)
318	**The Unthankful Are Always The Unhappy.**	**NOVEMBER 14** / *Acts 24-26* But avoid foolish questions, and genealogies, and contentions, and strivings about the law; for they are unprofitable and vain. (Titus 3:9)
319	**The Only Thing You Will Ever Need To Know Is What To Do Next.**	**NOVEMBER 15** / *Acts 27 - Romans 3* For unto us was the gospel preached, as well as unto them: but the word preached did not profit them, not being mixed with faith in them that heard it. (Hebrews 4:2)
320	**Your Future Is Decided By What You Are Willing To Change.**	**NOVEMBER 16** / *Romans 4-6* For the word of God is quick, and powerful, and sharper than any twoedged sword, piercing even to the dividing asunder of soul and spirit, and of the joints and marrow, and is a discerner of the thoughts and intents of the heart. (Hebrews 4:12)
321	**Those Pursuing Greatness Are Worthy Of Pursuit.**	**NOVEMBER 17** / *Romans 7-9* But now hath he obtained a more excellent ministry, by how much also he is the mediator of a better covenant, which was established upon better promises. (Hebrews 8:6)
322	**You Will Only Be Remembered For Your Obsession.**	**NOVEMBER 18** / *Romans 10-12* For this is the covenant that I will make with the house of Israel after those days, saith the Lord; I will put My laws into their mind, and write them in their hearts: and I will be to them a God, and they shall be to Me a people. (Hebrews 8:10)

WISDOM KEYS OF
MIKE MURDOCK ©

WISDOM KEY#	WISDOM KEY	MEMORY SCRIPTURES ON THE WORD OF GOD
323	The Person Of Jesus Prepares You For Eternity; The Principles Of Jesus Prepare You For Earth.	**NOVEMBER 19** / *Romans 13-15* And for this cause He is the mediator of the new testament, that by means of death, for the redemption of the transgressions that were under the first testament, they which are called might receive the promise of eternal inheritance. (Hebrews 9:15)
324	When You Get Involved With God's Family; He Will Get Involved With Your Family.	**NOVEMBER 20** / *Romans 16-1 Corinthians 2* This is the covenant that I will make with them after those days, saith the Lord, I will put My laws into their hearts, and in their minds will I write them. (Hebrews 10:16)
325	Those Who Cannot Increase You Will Inevitably Decrease You.	**NOVEMBER 21** / *1 Corinthians 3-5* Wherefore lay apart all filthiness and superfluity of naughtiness, and receive with meekness the engrafted word, which is able to save your souls. (James 1:21)
326	Loss Is The First Step Toward Discovering God.	**NOVEMBER 22** / *1 Corinthians 6-10* But be ye doers of the word, and not hearers only, deceiving your own selves. (James 1:22)
327	Your Goals Allow Your Friends To Confirm Their Loyalty.	**NOVEMBER 23** / *1 Corinthians 11-13* For if any be a hearer of the word, and not a doer, he is like unto a man beholding his natural face in a glass: For he beholdeth himself, and goeth his way, and straightway forgetteth what manner of man he was. (James 1:23,24)
328	Those Who Habitually Disagree With Your Decisions Eventually Become Capable Of Disloyalty.	**NOVEMBER 24** / *1 Corinthians 14-16* But whoso looketh into the perfect law of liberty, and continueth therein, he being not a forgetful hearer, but a doer of the work, this man shall be blessed in his deed. (James 1:25)
329	Your Faith Decides Your Miracles.	**NOVEMBER 25** / *2 Corinthians 1-3* If ye fulfil the royal law according to the scripture, Thou shalt love thy neighbour as thyself, ye do well: (James 2:8)

WISDOM KEYS OF
MIKE MURDOCK©

WISDOM KEY#	WISDOM KEY	MEMORY SCRIPTURES ON THE WORD OF GOD
330	Greatness Is Simply Fulfilling God's Expectations Of You.	**NOVEMBER 26** / *2 Corinthians 4-6* For whosoever shall keep the whole law, and yet offend in one point, he is guilty of all. (James 2:10)
331	Those Who Disagree With Your Goals Will Usually Disagree With Your Decisions.	**NOVEMBER 27** / *2 Corinthians 7-9* Being born again, not of corruptible seed, but of incorruptible, by the word of God, which liveth and abideth for ever. (1 Peter 1:23)
332	Those Who Sin With You Will Eventually Sin Against You.	**NOVEMBER 28** / *2 Corinthians 10-12* But the word of the Lord endureth for ever. And this is the word which by the gospel is preached unto you. (1 Peter 1:25)
333	You Are Never As Far From A Miracle As It First Appears.	**NOVEMBER 29** / *2 Corinthians 13-Galatians 4* As newborn babes, desire the sincere milk of the word, that ye may grow thereby. (1 Peter 2:2)
334	Your Self-Portrait Determines What You Are Willing To Endure.	**NOVEMBER 30** / *Galatians 5 - Ephesians 1* For the time is come that judgment must begin at the house of God: and if it first begin at us, what shall the end be of them that obey not the gospel of God? (1 Peter 4:17)
335	Intolerance Of Your Present Schedules Your Future.	**DECEMBER 1** / *Ephesians 2-4* Whereby are given unto us exceeding great and precious promises: that by these ye might be partakers of the divine nature, having escaped the corruption that is in the world through lust. (2 Peter 1:4)
336	Ecstasy To A Giver Is Discovering Someone Qualified To Receive.	**DECEMBER 2** / *Ephesians 5 - Philippians 1* We have also a more sure word of prophecy; whereunto ye do well that ye take heed, as unto a light that shineth in a dark place, until the day dawn, and the day star arise in your hearts. (2 Peter 1:19)

WISDOM KEYS OF
MIKE MURDOCK©

WISDOM KEY#	WISDOM KEY	MEMORY SCRIPTURES ON THE WORD OF GOD
337	**Order Is Simply The Accurate Arrangement Of Things.**	**DECEMBER 3** / *Philippians 2-4* Knowing this first, that no prophecy of the scripture is of any private interpretation. (2 Peter 1:20)
338	**An Uncommon Future Requires An Uncommon Mentor.**	**DECEMBER 4** / *Colossians 1-3* The Lord is not slack concerning His promise, as some men count slackness; but is longsuffering to us-ward, not willing that any should perish, but that all should come to repentance. (2 Peter 3:9)
339	**What You Love Will Eventually Reward You.**	**DECEMBER 5** / *Colossians 4-1 Thessalonians 2* As also in all His epistles, speaking in them of these things; in which are some things hard to be understood, which they that are unlearned and unstable wrest, as they do also the other scriptures, unto their own destruction. (2 Peter 3:16)
340	**You Can Only Conquer Something You Hate.**	**DECEMBER 6** / *1 Thessalonians 3 - 2 Thessalonians 2* For the prophecy came not in old time by the will of man: but holy men of God spake as they were moved by the Holy Ghost. (2 Peter 1:21)
341	**The Proof Of Impatience Is Debt.**	**DECEMBER 7** / *2 Thessalonians 3 - 1 Timothy 2* This then is the message which we have heard of Him, and declare unto you, that God is light, and in Him is no darkness at all. (1 John 1:5)
342	**Champions Make Decisions That Create The Future They Desire; Losers Make Decisions That Create The Present They Desire.**	**DECEMBER 8** / *1 Timothy 3-5* If we say that we have not sinned, we make Him a liar, and His word is not in us. (1 John 1:10)
343	**Anything You Do In An Attempt To Please God Will Not Go Unrewarded.**	**DECEMBER 9** / *1 Timothy 6 - 2 Timothy 2* And hereby we do know that we know Him, if we keep His commandments. (1 John 2:3)

WISDOM KEYS OF
MIKE MURDOCK©

WISDOM KEY#	WISDOM KEY	MEMORY SCRIPTURES ON THE WORD OF GOD
344	Your Reaction To A Man Of God Determines God's Reaction To You.	**DECEMBER 10** / *2 Timothy 3 - Titus 1* He that saith, I know Him, and keepeth not His commandments, is a liar, and the truth is not in him. (1 John 2:4)
345	God Will Never Advance Your Instructions Beyond Your Last Act Of Disobedience.	**DECEMBER 11** / *Titus 2 - Philemon 1* But whoso keepeth His word, in him verily is the love of God perfected: hereby know we that we are in Him. (1 John 2:5)
346	Those Who Lie For You Will Eventually Lie Against You.	**DECEMBER 12** / *Hebrews 1-3* Again, a new commandment I write unto you, which thing is true in Him and in you: because the darkness is past, and the true light now shineth. (1 John 2:8)
347	When God Wants To Bless You, He Brings A Person Into Your Life.	**DECEMBER 13** / *Hebrews 4-8* I have written unto you, fathers, because ye have known Him that is from the beginning. I have written unto you, young men, because ye are strong, and the word of God abideth in you, and ye have overcome the wicked one. (1 John 2:14)
348	Your Pain Decides Your Goals.	**DECEMBER 14** / *Hebrews 9-11* And the world passeth away, and the lust thereof: but he that doeth the will of God abideth for ever. (1 John 2:17)
349	Your Memory Replays Your Past; Your Imagination Pre-Plays Your Future.	**DECEMBER 15** / *Hebrews 12 - James 1* Whosoever committeth sin transgresseth also the law: for sin is the transgression of the law. (1 John 3:4)
350	If You Must Believe Somebody, Believe Somebody Good.	**DECEMBER 16** / *James 2-4* And whatsoever we ask, we receive of Him, because we keep His commandments, and do those things that are pleasing in His sight. (1 John 3:22)

WISDOM KEYS OF
MIKE MURDOCK ©

WISDOM KEY#	WISDOM KEY	MEMORY SCRIPTURES ON THE WORD OF GOD
351	An Uncommon Future Will Require Uncommon Preparation.	**DECEMBER 17** / *James 5 - 1 Peter 2* And this is His commandment, That we should believe on the name of His Son Jesus Christ, and love one another, as He gave us commandment. (1 John 3:23)
352	Your Reaction To An Instruction Determines The Access You Receive.	**DECEMBER 18** / *1 Peter 3-5* And he that keepeth His commandments dwelleth in him, and He in him. And hereby we know that he abideth in us, by the Spirit which He hath given us. (1 John 3:24)
353	Those Who Do Not Respect Your Time Will Not Respect Your Wisdom Either.	**DECEMBER 19** / *2 Peter 1-3* And this commandment have we from Him, That he who loveth God love his brother also. (1 John 4:21)
354	When God Wants To Protect You, He Removes A Person From Your Life.	**DECEMBER 20** / *1 John 1-5* By this we know that we love the children of God, when we love God, and keep His commandments. (1 John 5:2)
355	Your Unwillingness To Submit Deprives God Of The Authorization To Protect.	**DECEMBER 21** / *2 John 1 - Jude 1* For this is the love of God, that we keep His commandments: and His commandments are not grievous. (1 John 5:3)
356	Those Without Your Pain Never Understand Your Goals.	**DECEMBER 22** / *Revelation 1-3* For there are three that bear record in heaven, the Father, the Word, and the Holy Ghost: and these three are one. (1 John 5:7)
357	An Uncommon Dream Requires Uncommon Faith.	**DECEMBER 23** / *Revelation 4-5* And this is love, that we walk after His commandments. This is the commandment, That, as ye have heard from the beginning, ye should walk in it. (2 John 1:6)

WISDOM KEYS OF
MIKE MURDOCK ©

WISDOM KEY#	WISDOM KEY	MEMORY SCRIPTURES ON THE WORD OF GOD
358	What You Celebrate— You Will Remember.	**DECEMBER 24** / *Revelation 6-7* Whosoever transgresseth, and abideth not in the doctrine of Christ, hath not God. He that abideth in the doctrine of Christ, he hath both the Father and the Son. (2 John 1:9)
359	The Most Valuable Person In Your Life Is The One Who Feeds Your Faith.	**DECEMBER 25** / *Revelation 8-9* Blessed is he that readeth, and they that hear the words of this prophecy, and keep those things which are written therein: for the time is at hand. (Revelation 1:3)
360	Those Who Disrespect Your Assignment Are Unqualified For Access.	**DECEMBER 26** / *Revelation 10-11* And He was clothed with a vesture dipped in blood: and His name is called The Word of God. (Revelation 19:13)
361	When You Agree With A Rebel, You Reap His Consequences.	**DECEMBER 27** / *Revelation 12-16* Behold, I come quickly: blessed is he that keepeth the sayings of the prophecy of this book. (Revelation 22:7)
362	Your Experiences Decide Your Persuasions.	**DECEMBER 28** / *Revelation 17-18* Blessed are they that do His commandments, that they may have right to the tree of life, and may enter in through the gates into the city. (Revelation 22:14)
363	Your Reaction To Someone In Trouble Determines God's Reaction To You.	**DECEMBER 29** / *Revelation 19-20* For I testify unto every man that heareth the words of the prophecy of this book, If any man shall add unto these things, God shall add unto him the plagues that are written in this book. (Revelation 22:18)
364	What You Can Walk Away From You Have Mastered; What You Cannot Walk Away From Has Mastered You.	**DECEMBER 30** / *Revelation 21-22* And He that sat upon the throne said, Behold, I make all things new. And He said unto me, Write: for these words are true and faithful. (Revelation 21:5)
365	Anything Broken Can Be Repaired; Anything Closed Can Be Opened; Anything Lost Can Be Recovered.	**DECEMBER 31** / *Well Done!* And if any man shall take away from the words of the book of this prophecy, God shall take away his part out of the book of life, and out of the holy city, and from the things which are written in this book. (Revelation 22:19)

31 FACTS ABOUT WISDOM

1. Wisdom Is The Master Key To All The Treasures Of Life.
2. Wisdom Is A Gift From God To You.
3. The Fear Of God Is The Beginning Of Wisdom.
4. The Wisdom Of This World Is A False Substitute For The Wisdom Of God.
5. The Wisdom Of Man Is Foolishness To God.
6. Right Relationships Increase Your Wisdom.
7. The Wisdom Of God Is Foolishness To The Natural Mind.
8. Your Conversation Reveals How Much Wisdom You Possess.
9. Jesus Is Made Unto Us Wisdom.
10. All The Treasures Of Wisdom And Knowledge Are Hid In Jesus Christ.
11. The Word Of God Is Your Source Of Wisdom.
12. God Will Give You Wisdom When You Take The Time To Listen.
13. The Word Of God Is Able To Make You Wise Unto Salvation.
14. The Holy Spirit Is The Spirit Of Wisdom That Unleashes Your Gifts, Talents And Skills.
15. Men Of Wisdom Will Always Be Men Of Mercy.
16. Wisdom Is Better Than Jewels Or Money.
17. Wisdom Is More Powerful Than Weapons Of War.
18. He That Wins Souls Is Wise.
19. The Wise Hate Evil And The Evil Hate The Wise.

20. Wisdom Reveals The Treasure In Yourself.
21. The Proof Of Wisdom Is The Presence Of Joy And Peace.
22. Wisdom Makes Your Enemies Helpless Against You.
23. Wisdom Creates Currents Of Favor And Recognition Toward You.
24. The Wise Welcome Correction.
25. When The Wise Speak, Healing Flows.
26. When You Increase Your Wisdom You Will Increase Your Wealth.
27. Wisdom Can Be Imparted By The Laying On Of Hands Of A Man Of God.
28. Wisdom Guarantees Promotion.
29. Wisdom Loves Those Who Love Her.
30. Wisdom Will Be Given To You When You Pray For It In Faith.
31. The Mantle Of Wisdom Makes You 10 Times Stronger Than Those Without It.

$\mathcal{T}$OPIC

$\mathcal{T}$HOUGHT

DATE:

Choice Is The Divine Paint Brush God Gives
Every Man To Design His Own World.

-MIKE MURDOCK

$\mathscr{T}$OPIC $\mathscr{T}$HOUGHT

DATE:

What You Do Daily Determines
What You Become Permanently.
                    -MIKE MURDOCK

${\mathcal{T}}$OPIC

DATE:

${\mathcal{T}}$HOUGHT

The Secret Of Your Future
Is Hidden In Your Daily Routine.
                    -MIKE MURDOCK

$\mathcal{T}$OPIC

$\mathcal{T}$HOUGHT

DATE:

Distractions Only Occur With Your Permission.

-MIKE MURDOCK

DECISION

Will You Accept Jesus As Your Personal Savior Today?

The Bible says, That if thou shalt confess with thy mouth the Lord Jesus, and shalt believe in thine heart that God hath raised Him from the dead, thou shalt be saved (Romans 10:9).

Pray this prayer from your heart today!

Dear Jesus, I believe that You died for me and rose again on the third day. I confess I am a sinner...I need Your love and forgiveness...Come into my heart. Forgive my sins. I receive Your eternal life. Confirm Your love by giving me peace, joy and supernatural love for others. Amen.

☐ Yes, Mike! I made a decision to accept Christ as my personal Savior today. Please send me my free gift of your book, *31 Keys to a New Beginning* to help me with my new life in Christ. *(B-48)*

Clip and Mail

NAME _____ BIRTHDAY _____

ADDRESS _____

CITY _____ STATE _____ ZIP _____

PHONE _____ E-MAIL _____

Mail form to:
    The Wisdom Center · *4051 Denton Hwy.* · *Ft. Worth, TX 76117*
    1-888-WISDOM-1 (1-817-759-0300) · **Website:** *TheWisdomCenter.tv*

Unless otherwise indicated, all Scripture quotations are taken from the King James Version of the Bible.
The Wisdom Key Devotional
ISBN 1-56394-256-9/B-165
Copyright © 2005 by **MIKE MURDOCK**
All publishing rights belong exclusively to Wisdom International
Publisher/Editor: Deborah Murdock Johnson
Published by The Wisdom Center · 4051 Denton Hwy. · Ft. Worth, Texas 76117
1-888-WISDOM-1 (1-817-759-0300) · **Website: TheWisdomCenter.tv**
1005

DR. MIKE MURDOCK

1 Has embraced his Assignment to Pursue...Proclaim...and Publish the Wisdom of God to help people achieve their dreams and goals.

2 Began full-time evangelism at the age of 19, which has continued since 1966.

3 Has traveled and spoken to more than 14,000 audiences in 39 countries, including East and West Africa, the Orient and Europe.

4 Noted author of over 160 books, including best sellers, Wisdom For Winning," Dream Seeds and The Double Diamond Principle.

5 Created the popular Topical Bible series for Businessmen, Mothers, Fathers, Teenagers; The One-Minute Pocket Bible series, and The Uncommon Life series.

6 Has composed more than 5,700 songs such as I Am Blessed," You Can Make It," God Rides On Wings Of Love and Jesus, Just The Mention Of Your Name," recorded by many gospel artists.

7 Is the Founder of The Wisdom Center, in Fort Worth, Texas.

8 Has a weekly television program called Wisdom Keys With Mike Murdock.

9 Has appeared often on TBN, CBN, BET and other television network programs.

10 Is a Founding Trustee on the Board of International Charismatic Bible Ministries with Oral Roberts.

11 Has had more than 3,500 accept the call into full-time ministry under his ministry.

THE MINISTRY

1 Wisdom Books & Literature - Over 160 best-selling Wisdom Books and 70 Teaching Tape Series.

2 Church Crusades - Multitudes are ministered to in crusades and seminars throughout America in The Uncommon Wisdom Conferences. Known as a man who loves pastors he has focused on church crusades for 38 years.

3 Music Ministry - Millions have been blessed by the anointed songwriting and singing of Mike Murdock, who has made over 15 music albums and CDs available.

4 Television - *Wisdom Keys With Mike Murdock,"* a nationally-syndicated weekly television program.

5 The Wisdom Center - The Ministry offices where Schools of Wisdom have been held.

6 Schools of the Holy Spirit - Mike Murdock hosts Schools of the Holy Spirit in many churches to mentor believers on the Person and Companionship of the Holy Spirit.

7 Schools of Wisdom - In many major cities Mike Murdock hosts Schools of Wisdom for those who want personalized and advanced training for achieving The Uncommon Life.

8 Missions Outreach - Dr. Mike Murdock's overseas outreaches to 39 countries have included crusades in East and West Africa, South America, the Orient and Europe.

2005

January
S	M	T	W	T	F	S
						1
2	3	4	5	6	7	8
9	10	11	12	13	14	15
16	17	18	19	20	21	22
23	24	25	26	27	28	29
30	31					

February
S	M	T	W	T	F	S
		1	2	3	4	5
6	7	8	9	10	11	12
13	14	15	16	17	18	19
20	21	22	23	24	25	26
27	28					

March
S	M	T	W	T	F	S
		1	2	3	4	5
6	7	8	9	10	11	12
13	14	15	16	17	18	19
20	21	22	23	24	25	26
27	28	29	30	31		

April
S	M	T	W	T	F	S
					1	2
3	4	5	6	7	8	9
10	11	12	13	14	15	16
17	18	19	20	21	22	23
24	25	26	27	28	29	30

May
S	M	T	W	T	F	S
1	2	3	4	5	6	7
8	9	10	11	12	13	14
15	16	17	18	19	20	21
22	23	24	25	26	27	28
29	30	31				

June
S	M	T	W	T	F	S
			1	2	3	4
5	6	7	8	9	10	11
12	13	14	15	16	17	18
19	20	21	22	23	24	25
26	27	28	29	30		

July
S	M	T	W	T	F	S
					1	2
3	4	5	6	7	8	9
10	11	12	13	14	15	16
17	18	19	20	21	22	23
24	25	26	27	28	29	30
31						

August
S	M	T	W	T	F	S
	1	2	3	4	5	6
7	8	9	10	11	12	13
14	15	16	17	18	19	20
21	22	23	24	25	26	27
28	29	30	31			

September
S	M	T	W	T	F	S
				1	2	3
4	5	6	7	8	9	10
11	12	13	14	15	16	17
18	19	20	21	22	23	24
25	26	27	28	29	30	

October
S	M	T	W	T	F	S
						1
2	3	4	5	6	7	8
9	10	11	12	13	14	15
16	17	18	19	20	21	22
23	24	25	26	27	28	29
30	31					

November
S	M	T	W	T	F	S
		1	2	3	4	5
6	7	8	9	10	11	12
13	14	15	16	17	18	19
20	21	22	23	24	25	26
27	28	29	30			

December
S	M	T	W	T	F	S
				1	2	3
4	5	6	7	8	9	10
11	12	13	14	15	16	17
18	19	20	21	22	23	24
25	26	27	28	29	30	31

2006

January
S	M	T	W	T	F	S
1	2	3	4	5	6	7
8	9	10	11	12	13	14
15	16	17	18	19	20	21
22	23	24	25	26	27	28
29	30	31				

February
S	M	T	W	T	F	S
			1	2	3	4
5	6	7	8	9	10	11
12	13	14	15	16	17	18
19	20	21	22	23	24	25
26	27	28				

March
S	M	T	W	T	F	S
			1	2	3	4
5	6	7	8	9	10	11
12	13	14	15	16	17	18
19	20	21	22	23	24	25
26	27	28	29	30	31	

April
S	M	T	W	T	F	S
						1
2	3	4	5	6	7	8
9	10	11	12	13	14	15
16	17	18	19	20	21	22
23	24	25	26	27	28	29
30						

May
S	M	T	W	T	F	S
	1	2	3	4	5	6
7	8	9	10	11	12	13
14	15	16	17	18	19	20
21	22	23	24	25	26	27
28	29	30	31			

June
S	M	T	W	T	F	S
				1	2	3
4	5	6	7	8	9	10
11	12	13	14	15	16	17
18	19	20	21	22	23	24
25	26	27	28	29	30	

July
S	M	T	W	T	F	S
						1
2	3	4	5	6	7	8
9	10	11	12	13	14	15
16	17	18	19	20	21	22
23	24	25	26	27	28	29
30	31					

August
S	M	T	W	T	F	S
		1	2	3	4	5
6	7	8	9	10	11	12
13	14	15	16	17	18	19
20	21	22	23	24	25	26
27	28	29	30	31		

September
S	M	T	W	T	F	S
					1	2
3	4	5	6	7	8	9
10	11	12	13	14	15	16
17	18	19	20	21	22	23
24	25	26	27	28	29	30

October
S	M	T	W	T	F	S
1	2	3	4	5	6	7
8	9	10	11	12	13	14
15	16	17	18	19	20	21
22	23	24	25	26	27	28
29	30	31				

November
S	M	T	W	T	F	S
			1	2	3	4
5	6	7	8	9	10	11
12	13	14	15	16	17	18
19	20	21	22	23	24	25
26	27	28	29	30		

December
S	M	T	W	T	F	S
					1	2
3	4	5	6	7	8	9
10	11	12	13	14	15	16
17	18	19	20	21	22	23
24	25	26	27	28	29	30
31						

FOR *Fathers* ONLY!

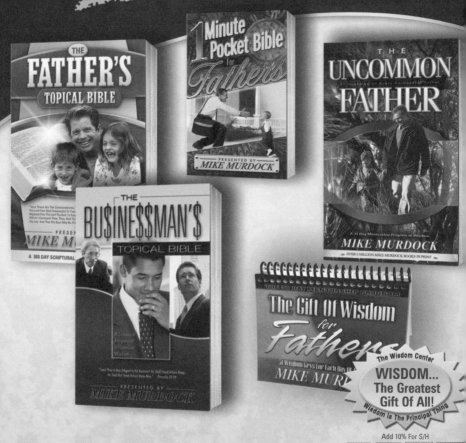

Add 10% For S/H

WISDOM... The Greatest Gift Of All!

The Wisdom Center

Wisdom Is The Principal Thing

❶ **The Father's Topical Bible**/<u>Book</u> (378pg/B-35/$10)

❷ **1 Minute Pocket Bible For Fathers**/<u>Book</u> (130pg/B-51/$5)

❸ **The Uncommon Father**/<u>Book</u> (176pg/B-131/$10)

❹ **The Businessman's Topical Bible**/<u>Book</u> (383pg/B-33/$10)

❺ **The Gift of Wisdom for Fathers**/<u>Book</u> (32pg/B-77/$10)

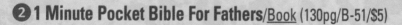

THE WISDOM CENTER **1-888-WISDOM-1**
4051 Denton Highway • Fort Worth, TX 76117 **1-817-759-0300**

Website:
TheWisdomCenter.tv

Quantity Prices Available Upon Request

FOR *Mothers* ONLY!

1 **1 Minute Pocket Bible For Mothers**/<u>Book</u> (132pg/B-52/$5)

2 **The Mother's Topical Bible**/<u>Book</u> (468pg/B-36/$10)

3 **The Proverbs 31 Woman**/<u>Book</u> (70pg/B-49/$7)

4 **The Uncommon Mother**/<u>Book</u> (174pg/B-132/$10)

5 **Thirty-One Secrets of an Unforgettable Woman**/<u>Book</u> (140pg/B-57/$9)

6 **The Gift of Wisdom for Mothers**/<u>Book</u> (32pg/B-70/$10)

THE WISDOM CENTER **1-888-WISDOM-1**
WISDOM CENTER 4051 Denton Highway • Fort Worth, TX 76117 **1-817-759-0300**

Website:
TheWisdomCenter.tv

Quantity Prices Available Upon Request

ESPECIALLY FOR *Teens!*

① **Finding Your Purpose In Life**/<u>Book</u> (32pg/B-05/$3)

② **How To Turn Your Mistakes Into Miracles**/<u>Book</u> (32pg/B-56/$5)

③ **1 Minute Pocket Bible For Teenagers**/<u>Book</u> (124pg/B-53/$5)

④ **Seeds of Wisdom on Enemies**/<u>Book</u> (32pg/B-124/$5)

⑤ **Seeds of Wisdom on Goal-Setting**/<u>Book</u> (32pg/B-127/$5)

⑥ **Seeds of Wisdom on Problem-Solving**/<u>Book</u> (32pg/B-118/$5)

⑦ **Seeds of Wisdom on Relationships**/<u>Book</u> (32pg/B-14/$3)

⑧ **The Sex Trap**/<u>Book</u> (32pg/B-03/$3)

⑨ **The Teen's Topical Bible**/<u>Book</u> (436pg/B-30/$10)

⑩ **Wisdom For Winning**/<u>Book</u> (226pg/B-01/$10)

⑪ **The Gift of Wisdom for Teenagers**/<u>Book</u> (32pg/B-85/$10)

The Wisdom Center

All 11 Books for only
$66
WBL-31

Wisdom Is The Principal Thing

Add 10% For S/H

*This offer expires December 31, 2006. **Each Wisdom Book may be purchased separately if so desired.*

THE WISDOM CENTER 1-888-WISDOM-1
4051 Denton Highway • Fort Worth, TX 76117   1-817-759-0300

Website:
TheWisdomCenter.tv

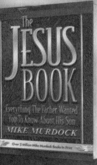

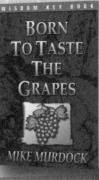

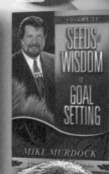

Career 7

❶ **The Businessman's Topical Bible**/<u>Book</u> (384pg/B-33/$10)

❷ **31 Secrets For Career Success**/<u>Book</u> (114pg/B-44/$10)

❸ **31 Scriptures Every Businessman Should Memorize**/<u>Book</u> (32pg/B-141/$3)

❹ **Seeds Of Wisdom On Goal-Setting** /<u>Book</u> (32pg/B-127/$5)

❺ **Seeds Of Wisdom On Problem-Solving** /<u>Book</u> (32pg/B-118/$5)

❻ **Seeds Of Wisdom On Productivity**/<u>Book</u> (32pg/B-137/$5)

❼ **The Mentor's Manna On Achievement**/<u>Book</u> (32pg/B-79/$3)

Each book may be purchased separately if so desired.

DR. MIKE MURDOCK

The Wisdom Center
Only **$30!**
Retail Value $41
WBL-27
Wisdom Is The Principal Thing

Add 10% For S/H

THE **WISDOM CENTER** 1-888-WISDOM-1
4051 Denton Highway • Fort Worth, TX 76117 1-817-759-0300

Website:
TheWisdomCenter.tv

*This offer expires December 31, 2005

101 Wisdom Keys That Have Most Changed My Life.

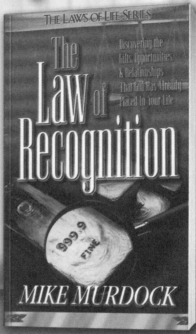

TS-42

School of Wisdom #2

- ▶ What Attracts Others Toward You
- ▶ The Secret Of Multiplying Your Financial Blessings
- ▶ What Stops The Flow Of Your Faith
- ▶ Why Some Fail And Others Succeed
- ▶ How To Discern Your Life Assignment
- ▶ How To Create Currents Of Favor With Others
- ▶ How To Defeat Loneliness
- ▶ 47 Keys In Recognizing The Mate God Has Approved For You
- ▶ 14 Facts You Should Know About Your Gifts And Talents
- ▶ 17 Important Facts You Should Remember About Your Weakness
- ▶ And Much, Much More...

WISDOM CENTER — **THE WISDOM CENTER** **1-888-WISDOM-1**
4051 Denton Highway • Fort Worth, TX 76117   **1-817-759-0300**

Website:
TheWisdomCenter.tv

This offer expires December 31, 2005

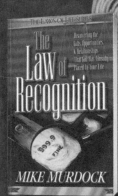
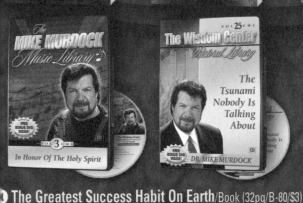

The CRISIS COLLECTION

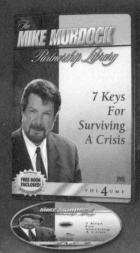
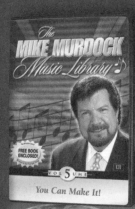

You Get All 6 For One Great Price!

① **7 Keys For Surviving A Crisis**/DVD (MMPL-04D/$10)

② **You Can Make It!**/Music CD (MMML-05/$10)

③ **Wisdom For Crisis Times**/6 Cassettes (TS-40/$30)

④ **Seeds of Wisdom on Overcoming**/Book (32pg/B-17/$3)

⑤ **Seeds of Wisdom on Motivating Yourself**/Book (32pg/B-171/$5)

⑥ **Wisdom For Crisis Times**/Book (112pg/B-40/$9)

Also Included... Two Free Bonus Books!

Each Book/CD/DVD/Tape Series... May Be Purchased Separately If So Desired!

THE WISDOM CENTER **THE WISDOM CENTER** **1-888-WISDOM-1**
4051 Denton Highway • Fort Worth, TX 76117 **1-817-759-0300**

Website: **TheWisdomCenter.tv**

*This offer expires December 31, 2005

THE *TURNAROUND* Collection

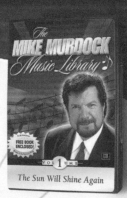

① 7 Keys To Turning Your Life Around
/DVD (MMPL-03D/$10)

② Battle Techniques For War Weary Saints/Book (32pg/B-07/$5)

③ Seeds Of Wisdom On Overcoming
/Book (32pg/B-17/$3)

④ The Memory Bible On Healing
/Book (32pg/B-196/$3)

⑤ How To Turn Your Mistakes Into Miracles/Book (32pg/B-56/$5)

⑥ The Wisdom Commentary Vol. 1
/Book (256pg/52 Topics/B-136/$20)

⑦ The Sun Will Shine Again
/Music CD (MMML-01/$10)

The Wisdom Center
Only **$39!**
Retail Value $56
PAK-15
Wisdom Is The Principal Thing

Add 10% For S/H

Each Book/CD/DVD...May Be Purchased Seperately If So Desired!

THE WISDOM CENTER 1-888-WISDOM-1
4051 Denton Highway • Fort Worth, TX 76117   1-817-759-0300

Website:
TheWisdomCenter.tv

*This offer expires December 31, 2005

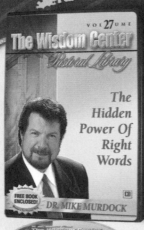
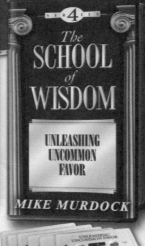

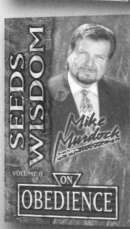

MY GIFT OF APPRECIATION...

The NEW Wisdom Commentary 2!

THE Mike Murdock COLLECTOR'S EDITION

THE WISDOM COMMENTARY 2

THIS NEW PAPERBACK VOLUME OF THE WISDOM COMMENTARY 2 INCLUDES 52 *DIFFERENT* TOPICS... FOR MENTORING YOUR FAMILY EVERY WEEK OF THE YEAR.

These topics include:

- Angels
- Anger
- Appearance
- Atmosphere
- Attitude
- Church
- Compassion
- Conversation
- Crisis
- Delegation
- Desire
- Disloyalty
- Distractions
- Expectation
- Failure
- Faith
- Faith-Talk
- Fasting
- Fathers
- Fear
- Focus
- Forgetting The Past
- Greatness
- Habits
- Humility
- Imagination
- Jealousy

- Marriage
- Mothers
- Motivating Yourself
- Negotiation
- Obedience
- Opportunity
- Order
- Overcoming
- Passion
- Peace
- Planning
- Prayer Language
- Relationships
- Respect
- Salvation
- Servanthood
- Singing
- Spiritual Warfare
- Submission
- Talents and Skills
- Tithing
- Unthankfulness
- Voice of God
- Vows
- Waiting on God

My Gift Of Appreciation To My Sponsors!...Those Who Sponsor Two Square Feet In The Completion Of The Wisdom Center!

Thank you so much for becoming a part of this wonderful project...The completion of The Wisdom Center! The total purchase and renovation cost of this facility (135,000 square feet) is over $6,000,000. This is approximately $100 for every two square feet. **The Wisdom Commentary is my Gift of Appreciation for your Sponsorship Seed of $100...that sponsors two square feet of The Wisdom Center. Become a Sponsor!** You will love this Volume 2, of The Wisdom Commentary. It is my exclusive Gift of Appreciation for those who partner with me in the Work of God as a Sponsor.

THE Financial 7 Book PAK

① **Secrets Of The Richest Man Who Ever Lived**/<u>Book</u> (180pg/B-99/$10)

② **7 Keys To 1000 Times More**/<u>Book</u> (126pg/B-104/$10)

③ **31 Reasons People Do Not Receive Their Financial Harvest**/<u>Book</u> (252pg/B-82/$12)

④ **Secrets Of The Journey, Vol. 3**/<u>Book</u> (32pg/B-94/$5)

⑤ **Secrets Of The Journey, Vol. 6**/<u>Book</u> (32pg/B-102/$5)

⑥ **Secrets Of The Journey, Vol. 7**/<u>Book</u> (32pg/B-103/$5)

⑦ **The Covenant Of 58 Blessings**/<u>Book</u> (82pg/B-47/$8)

Each book may be purchased separately if so desired.

THE WISDOM CENTER 4051 Denton Highway • Fort Worth, TX 76117
1-888-WISDOM-1
1-817-759-0300

Website:
TheWisdomCenter.tv

This offer expires December 31, 2005

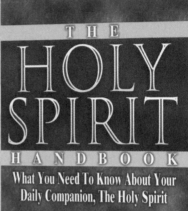

JOIN THE
Wisdom Key 3000
TODAY!

Dear Partner,

God has connected us!

I have asked the Holy Spirit for 3000 Special Partners who will plant a monthly Seed of $58.00 to help me bring the gospel around the world. (58 represents 58 kinds of blessings in the Bible.)

Will you become my monthly Faith Partner in The Wisdom Key 3000? Your monthly Seed of $58.00 is so powerful in helping heal broken lives. When you sow into the work of God, 4 Miracle Harvests are guaranteed in Scripture:

- ► Uncommon Protection (Mal. 3:10,11)
- ► Uncommon Favor (Lk. 6:38)
- ► Uncommon Health (Isa. 58:8)
- ► Financial Ideas and Wisdom (Deut. 8:18)

Your Faith Partner,

Mike Murdock
